LISTEN TO THE CHILDREN

D1372337

LISTEN TO THE CHILDREN

How empowering students can fix our broken schools

STACY PULICE, PH.D.

Weeping Willow Books

Listen to the Children
© 2018 Stacy Pulice, Ph.D.

Weeping Willow Books
Santa Barbara, California
www.weepingwillowbooks.com

Interior and cover design by Don Mitchell
Cover image by Shutterstock.com

ISBN 978-0-9990994-6-9

CONTENTS

PREFACE

A DREAM IN WINTER 2006 stands out as the beginning of my conscious journey into education and the child's psyche.

> In an auditorium, I am speaking to a large group of kids and adults. I reveal my vulnerability, using humor to put everyone at ease. Afterward, I go into the principal's office and sit down, announcing, "I want to learn how to work with kids who are gifted and different. I want to help, but I need to be taught the system for working with them." I begin to cry. "This is touching on my core issue—my desire to teach and actually reach kids—but I don't know how." The principal laughs, stating that there is no system for this. "I saw you get up in front of those people," she explains, "and I suggested you do that because I knew you could. Just get out there and do it." At that point, a familiar, sweet-looking, redheaded woman comes into the room, holding a two- to three-month-old baby girl on her hip. The baby, with wispy red hair and wearing a red-and-white dress, offers a

big smile. Her mom hands her to me. As I walk around the room with her, I tune in deeply to this precious child. She coos at me. Suddenly I realize that I can understand her baby-words. She is singing, "Love, love, love," mimicking the melody of The Beatles song, "All You Need Is Love." I show the mother and the principal the innate wisdom and intelligence of this baby. I feel happy and confident; I know how to do this. (Personal journal, 2006)

For me, there remains a clear sense of possibility based on the dream baby girl's song: "Love, love, love." In the co-created field of love, there is exchange. I learn about you and you learn about me. In that exchange of information, both verbal and non-verbal, we expand our insights, knowledge, and vision for the world in which we live. We create a shared experience that is the field of *philologia*, which invokes the passions of empathy, presence, and respect. It speaks of an I-Thou relationship—a deep communion—resembling the Hindu greeting, namaste: the divine in me greets the divine in you.

This subject came to me with tremendous passion, even numinosity, and I have since wrestled with the sense and meaning of it. I believe we are not here to help children. An attitude of rescuing reinforces a mindset based on colonizing others. We must instead see our efforts as crucial to both children and ourselves, and we must see them as partners in this effort. An observation from an Aboriginal Activist's Group, Queensland, 1970, feels relevant: "If you have come to help me you are wasting your time. But if you come because your liberation is bound up with mine, then let us work together."

FOREWORD

FROM THE LAND most Americans live on to the laws that protect their human and civil rights, colonial appropriation and logic have played a fundamental role in shaping American society. Native American peoples were massacred and displaced by white colonial settlers for the purpose of building "A City Upon a Hill"—a new society for the benefit of European origin populations, a United States that would eventually be seen by some as a beacon of democracy and civilization. The development of America as an economic world power would have not been possible without slavery. Multitudes of Africans and African-Americans were robbed of their humanity, sold as objects for the economic benefit of white landowners. The cotton they picked and the buildings they constructed propelled the American economy into an industrial revolution. America, as an empire, expanded West, stealing Native and Mexican land and turning population after population into exploitable, de-humanized, cheap labor. Even the very idea of the Constitution, one of America's pillars of democracy, was appropriated from Iroquois political philosophy.

Few white people today reflect on how colonization has produced so much wealth and privilege for Americans of European decent. Without the violent theft of Native land, white people would not own vast amounts of real estate; without black slavery, the institutions that white people benefit from, such as generational wealth transfers and the banking system, would not have accumulated surpluses of profit over centuries, allowing new generations to purchase property and expand wealth; without racist laws—lasting well through the 1960s—excluding non-whites from purchasing land or borrowing from banks—whites would not have such drastic control of the majority of real estate in communities of color; without Mexican low-wage workers, Americans would pay a lot more for services and products.

It is important for all Americans to understand the legacy of colonization and how it continues to impact historically oppressed peoples. It is also important to study the logic and practice of colonizing institutions; how they perpetuate modern-day colonization: how new generations learn it, *how children become colonized by systems of colonization in order to become the next generation of colonizers.* This is the contribution that Stacy Pulice makes in *Listen to the Children.* The author takes the reader on a journey through the pedagogical system of colonization, showing how it impacts the well-being of children and limits them in reaching their full human potential. Pulice helps us understand how the modern education system socializes children to learn to compete and produce profit at the cost of dehumanizing self and others. In participating in the process of dehumanization, the dehumanizer becomes detached from their humanity. In order to continue dehumanizing others for the sake of profit and privilege the oppressor must teach its offspring how to master this process. The only way to learn how to dehumanize others is by first being dehumanized, from a young age. One institution that plays a key role in teaching children how to dehumanize others is the education system.

Pulice uncovers how the American education system is set up to teach students more about academics and social Darwinist competition and less about becoming empathic critical thinkers and self-actualized human beings. In this process, children become alienated from their humanity— to be creative, to learn through play, to empathize with others, to build community, and to seek justice—and instead are taught to compete, to succeed at the cost of others, and to seek profit as a purpose in life. This is where Pulice's intrepid framework teaches readers how American education institutions have become colonizing institutions, even for white Americans. This makes sense, as to participate in the colonization of others one must first be colonized. Pulice impeccably demonstrates how regimented schools focused on test scores and academic outcomes create colonized children, even among the privileged classes.

Beyond showing the problems of our current education system, Pulice provides solutions. The author argues that we must focus on valuing the whole child. The whole child requires constant emotional support, opportunity for self-discovery, and social-justice-based learning. This model allows the education system to teach to the true humanity of the child: the empathic human, or as the author Jeremy Rifkin calls humanity at its full potential, "homo empathicus." That is, humans are wired to connect with others, to help others, to build community. At the very core of our nature, to be human is to be empathic; Pulice makes us take seriously the question, why not set up our education system to teach to this true humanity?

How can colonization be uprooted? We start with the colonizer. Once this population has been re-socialized, put in touch with its true humanity, decolonized, we will begin a true process of global peace, love, and human connection.

—Dr. Victor Rios, author, speaker, professor specializing in educational equity

INTRODUCTION

WHY TALK ABOUT COLONIZATION in the twenty-first century? That is something that happened long ago, to non-industrialized people in faraway lands, inflicted mostly by white Europeans of a time long past. But not by us and not today. The truth is, a colonizing mindset has permeated Western culture for hundreds of years, and we educate our children in its ways from an early age. The result of a colonizing mindset is self-alienation, competition for scarce opportunities and resources, racial segregation, and a repression of native wisdom that leaves young people with an increasing incidence of depression, anxiety, and toxic stress. Once an overt, brutal and violent hierarchical, institutional, fear-based, eat-or-be-eaten imperative, colonization has been softened, obfuscated, sugar-coated. Schools become primary institutions of socialization that subtly teach the next generation to either silence their protest or become little oppressors, seeing human competition and conflict as simply "the way it is."

This book examines the process by which children are harmed by the system we believe should provide them the greatest opportunity.

As a white middle-class woman, I experienced many privileges unseen by me or my peers. Even so, I have felt a sense of oppression that goes beyond being a woman in a patriarchal culture. Despite my higher education, I was plagued by an inability to fully express my thoughts and feelings, act independently and creatively, and feel safe to problem solve with imaginative freedom. I took this restriction for granted, assuming it was "just me," and found it to be grounds for lower self-esteem. But a fateful coincidence brought to the surface a previously invisible force that was oppressing my own children at the same time I was discovering my own expressive limits.

I returned to graduate school in the field of psychology— in a unique program where creativity, subjective experience, and the emotional, physical, and spiritual body are recognized as fundamental aspects of human experience, just as important as the logical, empirical, scientific, and dogmatic. It became a process of healing my own memories of oppression and subjugation in school. While I was participating in a more holistic classroom setting, my son was having quite a different experience in the local public grammar school. At age seven, he was being shamed for a wrong answer, and losing the privilege of going to recess and having a snack as a consequence of not raising his hand before answering a question.

Healing of the damage done to me as a child was running in time with current damage being done to him, and I wondered why my child was not receiving the same kind of education as I? Would he, too, have to wait years before entering a classroom where he was heard and seen, where his imagination was fostered and encouraged, and where his child's body wasn't restricted for hours every day to sitting in rows of desks? As he innocently framed it, "I think my teacher must have been raised in the Army." It dawned on me that children may be a marginalized, and potentially subjugated population, lacking both power and voice to create change.

This realization led to my dissertation research with teens where I found that, while knowing they didn't enjoy the dehumanizing process of public education, describing it alternately as "miserable, disrespectful, and unmotivating," they were grateful they had been prepared for "the real world." They were clear public schooling didn't offer true learning or character growth, but rather saw it as a painful institutional necessity, a stressful gauntlet that if you played the game well enough, would lead to a form of success, which was college. This contradiction confirms a degree of colonization.

To be clear, in using the term colonization, I do not want to suggest there is any comparison with the tragic loss of life, limb, language, and culture of so many populations in Africa, Indonesia, North and South America, just to name a few. The study of liberation psychology borrows the framework and dynamics of colonization and oppression of marginalized populations to point to an invisible yet pervasive appropriation of the autonomous community of children to reveal a subjugation that can be disabling to their creativity, self-esteem, and innate wisdom. I found a pervasive dehumanization cultivated in the *way* that we educate, thereby reducing children who go to school to that of a marginalized people, and those who teach them to a form of colonizer.

For some participants in my study, a love of learning was diminished by a process of memorizing large quantities of facts, repeating them back exactly, and then quickly forgetting. This style of curriculum, which they encountered at the public school, seeks statistical rates of performance over true learning, and was paradoxically viewed as "academic" by all. The development of loving relationships between students and teachers, known to be grease for the wheel of learning and so highly prized in some cultures, was all but eliminated. The fear of speaking truth to power, or giving the wrong answer, reduced risk-taking with learning. And imagination, which comes naturally to children as a form of creating the future, was captured for the retrospective act of memorization.

While my study participants were all young and female, two disempowered populations in the West, they were also white and middle class, demonstrating that oppression is present even for the privileged. In such a system, our culturally advantaged youth are socialized to become the next hegemony, adult perpetrators of a patriarchal culture that is familiar, and they ultimately become comfortable with the knowledge that this is the natural order of things. But there is a cost to society that affects both perceived winners and losers in the game of public education. Children are viewed as a colonized people, and additional categories of marginalization, such as gender, orientation, race, socioeconomics and ability, compound their lack of freedom, expression and opportunity.

Often studies of oppression are conducted with highly marginalized people, inner city kids who have disadvantages of race, poverty and opportunity; essentially groups who have nothing to lose. I was curious to know what issues remain in our public schools for children who have intact families, security and options. The girls in my study all attended a private school, some on scholarships, and lived in a beautiful community with natural amenities. They are some of the lucky ones who enjoy certain advantages. Sociologist Victor Rios conducted a two-year study at the same high school, with both male and female participants who were all Latino, many of whom have additional obstacles to success in public school. While the goal of his research was to discover the causes of the achievement gap in Latino students at the public high school, his findings were similar to mine. This tells us that essentially all people want the same things: to feel cared about, to feel respected and related to, to feel part of a community of learners, and to have opportunities and choices in their schooling to find success.

But we can learn from these kids what prevents them from performing better in public schools. Tragedy changes our brain and normal functioning. Trauma and toxic stress, exclusion and malnutrition, abuse and fear, all create a measurable drop in IQ and hijack our sense of well-being and purpose. You can't be curious if you mistrust; you can't be creative if you are hypervigilant. As Josh Aaronson said, fear makes you stupid. As our world gets more dangerous, and our kids have increased exposure to threats on multiple levels, our public schools must become the safest places in our communities. The key is asking children what they want and need, and then listening to them. What students told me in my study was that the presence of care, connection, community and choice made the difference between feeling engaged and motivated or feeling alienated and depressed. When a teacher at the public school provided these qualities, it enhanced the sense of humanity in the space, for both teachers and students, and kids were inspired to learn, explore and ask questions. When students' whole selves are treated with kindness in the classroom, and having loving relationships is more important than being right, children's minds expand and true learning can occur. Beyond our wildest dreams. So travel with me and I will show you how we can all benefit by liberating ourselves from a colonial mindset that keeps us from expressing our true genius.

A Dream Becomes a Passion

THE DREAM RECOUNTED in the prologue led to my search for what children who are "gifted and different" may be missing in school. What I discovered as a parent, and through my research in the field, is that all children are gifted, and they are all different. In a sense, we could all use special education, open instruction that meets us where we are and tells us how to interact with each other and with the world. We all crave the freedom to pursue what interests us and to express ourselves to others. And we all want to feel loved and safe. This definition of colonialism and its power clearly illustrated the essential dynamic I felt at play:

> Colonialism is based on two kinds of power. The first is the power of one group or individual to appropriate the resources, labor, and territory of another group or individual, creating hierarchy and inequality. The second power is

the capacity to deny responsibility for having done so, to silence resistance and opposition, and to normalize the outcome. [1]

Colonization often claims to be about helping others, either through creating viable trade from local resources or by civilizing indigenous savages. The outcome historically has resulted in the appropriation of the resources inherent in both the homelands and the human beings of less industrialized lands, often in service of the colonizing powers' own goals and profit. In such cases the colonizer has constructed an identity of Self and Other, creating a distinction between the dominant culture (me) versus the indigenous culture that is seen as Other (not me). Such a colonial mindset sets up the imposition of the dominant culture's extrinsic value system, beliefs, and customs onto those claimed to be in need of help or conversion as an unconscious way of justifying the abuse.

I began to question whether Western public education could be seen as a way the hegemonic adult population manages their constructed idea of the development of the indigenous person, in this case the child, requires. The indigenous child's natural resources of imaginative freedom, curiosity, inherent sense of play as a mode of learning, as well as emotional and physical openness may be harnessed, limited, and redirected through rote learning, memorization, and compliance. These creative and untamed qualities, universally found in children, are framed as invalid or inappropriate by current adult Western standards, and socialized out of them systematically in schools. By listening carefully to the experience of young

---

[1]Chapter 1Schulman-Lorenz & Watkins, 2003, p. 14

people who have been educated in both the standard public school system in my city as well as a private junior high school that specializes in holistic, humanistic education where priority is given to unconditional love and safe exploration, I hoped to better understand the effect our current Western system is having on children's sense of self, personal empowerment, and creative voice.

There is a term used in both sociology and psychology called Othering, which is a process of exclusion of and separation from others that happens at both the individual and group level, and has been seen as an important aspect of developing self-consciousness. Psychologically, our identity is closely connected with how we define the other, because a person understands his or her identity in relation to what he/she is not.[2] When this continues unchecked, it may play out at a societal level with a dominant population alienating or scapegoating a marginalized group. Rather than seeing those unlike us as complex beings with motivations, reflexes, priorities, emotions, and ideas of their own, we can easily dismiss them as being less valid, or to an extreme, less human, and not as worthy of respect and dignity as we are. In a colonizing environment, this entails identification of an indigenous population as an Other, a savage that requires transformative influence, and by the very nature of this Othering relationship, it precludes an empathic connection between Self and Other and can include cruelty and inhumanity in the name of civilization.

Othering can be used in both positive and negative ways. The first is Exclusionary Othering, which is a harmful process with dire consequences where power within

---

[2]Papadopoulos, 2002, p. 166

relationships is used for domination or subordination, and the Othered experiences alienation, marginalization, decreased opportunities, internalized oppression, and exclusion. The second is Inclusionary Othering, which utilizes power within relationships for transformation and coalition building. The constructive experience of Inclusionary Othering involves consciousness raising, sense of community, shared power, and inclusion. Difference is reconceptualized as a tool of creativity[3] for exploration, critique, and empowerment. It involves connecting with others as allies, and its ultimate goal is transformative growth for all.[4]

Colonizing forces utilize Exclusionary Othering to control and dictate to those being colonized. Throughout history, colonizing forces have overtaken indigenous populations that are often identifiable by physical characteristics such as skin color, their customs, dress, language, cultural norms, and beliefs. Colonizers have said, in their various languages: "Wear these clothes. Learn what's in this book. Use our language. Sit in rows in these schools. Observe our religion and beliefs." They have said: "We're here to help you. We're doing you a favor. We're going to get rid of everything that makes you a savage, and will make you better in the process." In many cases these hegemonic powers have actively suppressed and eliminated the traditions, beliefs, and cultural observances that once gave indigenous populations their sense of self and belonging in the world.

In public education, children are labeled as the Other, seen as existing in opposition to their adult counterparts.

[3]Selig, 2007
[4]Selig, 2007

Exclusionary Othering leans toward the colonial mindset of making children into a part of the adult world via oppression and indoctrination. Inclusionary Othering sees children more positively, embracing their inherent wisdom and teaching with an intention to encourage the full flowering of that wisdom.

In learning about the colonization and oppression of marginalized populations, I began to see how the language, philosophy, and behavior of colonialism appeared fully applicable to children, especially so in school. The classic literature in decolonial discourse never referred to children as a marginalized or oppressed group as such, and only referred to the colonized child in terms of racial, socioeconomic, or other secondary classifications to include them in the conversation. But as I grasped the definition of marginalized populations as those subject to social disadvantage and relegation to the fringe of society, the connection leapt out at me like a calling. Seen in the context of adult/child relationships, the population of children are effectively colonized by the adult population, and it is through this process that a marginalized group can be managed or made civilized. Children can be identified as being on a spectrum of oppression that holds the white European male adult at the apex of power, with women, people of color, and LGBTQ adults above children, who are just above animals in their humanity and rights.

Childhood in the West has been constructed by adults to be that which is not-adult, and as a result, children can be seen as Other and unlike the Self. Our current view of what constitutes the child is not a stable concept or one based only on a biological stage of life. It is, rather, a social and cultural construct that has changed radically over time. Childhood has been seen and described by the adult world as a process of becoming, with a highly local and fluid quality. Every aspect of childhood—their household responsibilities, play, schooling, relationships with parents and peers, and paths to adulthood—has changed over the past four centuries. The definitions and the experience of childhood vary according to changing cultural, demographic, economic, and historical circumstances.[5] While some less industrialized cultures still consider the lifespan of a human to be a continuum from birth to death, where they include their young in the labor and economic life of the family, many Western cultures define and construct a separate and bracketed element of life called childhood.

Children's subtle resources—psyche, mind, imagination, physical effort and future potential—are analogous to literal resources co-opted in colonial settings such as minerals, plants, labor, and territory. Children are identifiable via physical characteristics, as are indigenous people. When left to their own culture and social practices among peers, children possess their own perspective, knowing, skills, and insights not readily available to their adult counterparts. The ways in which we educate them can be considered tantamount to a subjugation and appropriation of the culture, belief systems and resources of children by the adult-oriented system. The ostensible purpose of this appropriation dates back to the Industrial Revolution, with the goal of creating assembly line workers and consumers who will support, take part in, and augment the current capitalistic, hierarchical systems that comprise

---

[5]Mintz, 2004, p. viii

consumerist societies. And we call this civilization. I would argue that children are educated in ways that suppress their natural gifts that may challenge current systems, to learn and think in unique ways, and to make choices that may not support the powers that currently sit at the apex of the power structure.

An overwhelming number of critiques have been undertaken within and across early childhood education, developmental psychology, history, and cultural studies that suggest that childhood is a cultural construction. The constructed child has alternately been reified by Rousseau as the Other, in the form of the Noble Savage, and denigrated by Hobbes as immoral and in need of imposing containment and civilization. Children are variously seen as innocent (i.e., simple, ignorant, not yet adult), dependent (i.e., needy, unable to speak for themselves, vulnerable, victims), and cute (i.e., objects, playthings, to be watched and discussed), all of which make them less than fully human in the adult view.[6]

As I realized the construction of Othering relationships, I arrived at the question: Are children in modern schools largely a colonized people? If so, how can we know this, and what damage might this be doing?

LIBERATION PSYCHOLOGY AND THE COLONIZED CHILD

I am using the frame of liberation psychology because several of its key terms aptly describe treatment of and regard for children in much of the industrialized Western

---

[6]Cannella & Kincheloe, 2002, p. 3

world: oppression, colonization, hegemony. Based on my research, my personal experience, the experience of my children, and that of the children of many parents I have spoken with, these are terms well-suited to the subject at hand. They may seem radical at first—after all, schools are places full of loving, caring people who are trying to provide the best possible education for children. The United States is among the fortunate nations with free, mandated public education that provides opportunity for all, an advantage that is significant by any measure. Dare we ask if this system is oppressive when it has done so much good? Yes. I believe it is well worth investigating if children encounter a destructive power dynamic in the current Western educational system, a dynamic that has been thoroughly identified and addressed within the field of liberation psychology.

This pervasive authoritarian influence extends into the language spoken within a colonizing hegemony in order to normalize its inherent domination. Several forms of discourse reveal how children can be oppressed by the ways in which they are spoken to, about, depicted, and encultured. Colonial discourse identifies a colonized or primitive people as closer to the animal world, and presents this identification as entirely "natural," as a simple state of what is, rather than as a determination made to benefit the interests of those doing the colonizing.[7] Sociologist David Spurr, in *The Rhetoric of Empire*, explored language as "colonial discourse"[8] and offered examples of twelve ways in which language oppresses. For example, there is the language of Appropriation, wherein a "colonized people is

[7]Spurr, 1993, p. 157
[8]David Spurr, 1993, p. 157

morally improved and edified,"[9] deemed as innocent and therefore ripe for instruction. Although Spurr related this to non-Western cultures, this can be regarded from the perspective of children and their educational experiences as well. When seen as a way of managing the development of the child, education can also negate that child's inborn knowledge-base and culture, considering it invalid and inappropriate to current standards of value. Even the field of child development is the creation of the adult, who presupposes the goals of childhood to fit their ideas of who they should become and at what pace.

Negation is another form of colonial discourse where the Other is equated with "absence, emptiness, and nothingness."[10] Negation is not a matter of conquest, but deliverance, and it is up to the instructor to deliver the child out of his or her ignorance, and into the hands of an established worldview. This supposed rescue into adulthood is done regardless of the fact that this worldview is counterintuitive to the imaginative child and to the child who is still immersed in the truth of a nature-infused reality.

Affirmation, or validation of the speaking subject's authority through his or her "moral superiority"[11] offers a glimpse into the ways adult language can affect the child's freedom of imagination. Simply, the adult parent/teacher is morally superior to the wild child by mere function of the elevated language he or she uses. This very way of speaking, perhaps deliberately above the intellectual capability of the child, enhances an oppressive move. Children's creative

[9]Spurr, 1993, p. 33
[10]Spurr, 1993, p. 92
[11]Spurr, 1993, p. 110

use of words, make believe, and more limited vocabulary are cause to view them as inferior to adults.

Children can be seen as an oppressed population, with the school system acting as the oppressor. Oppression in this case takes form as suppression of creativity, stifling of imagination/expression of self, and reduced ability to form relationships. This subtle erosion of personal voice and power sets up a vulnerability to other forms of oppression when poverty, racism, or gender/orientation subordination are present. In considering the issues involved in empowering children, we can learn a great deal from other anti-oppressive movements, such as the Civil Rights Movement of the 1950s and 60s, LGBT movements of the twentieth century, and the Women's Movement, which began in 1848, all of which continue their struggles to the current day. The United Nations declared the Convention of the Rights of the Child in 1989, which defines their human rights to care and nurturing, and freedom from abuse. All human rights struggles include similar forces of repression, devaluation, and inequality. In her writings on patriarchy and feminist resistance, Kathleen A. Barry, Ph.D. described the way in which patriarchal tenets "infect women's intrapsychic spaces and content, their interpersonal relationships, and the institutions that frame their lives."[12] This is where all forms of oppression have their deepest impact: in transforming the oppressed into entities who shape themselves to suit the needs of their oppressors because they know no other way of being. Awakening to hegemony is a process not only of seeing oppression from without, but also recognizing how we

---

[12] Kathleen A. Barry, Ph.D. 2010, pp. 17-18

have internalized that oppression, allowing it to shape our thoughts, relationships, and ways of participating in the world. In his October 2003 keynote address to the Alaskan Federation of Natives Convention, Māori academic Graham Hingangaroa Smith stated:

> Hegemony is a way of thinking—it occurs when oppressed groups take on dominant-group thinking and ideas uncritically and as "common-sense," even though those ideas may in fact be contributing to forming their own oppression. It is the ultimate way to colonize a people; you have the colonized colonizing themselves! [13]

While exploring roots of the oppression children were experiencing in the classroom, I began with an assumption that the problem stemmed from teachers with power trips. What I found was that hierarchical power is part of the Western thought system and that it reaches far beyond the parent, the teacher, and the administrator. It is woven indelibly into our belief system of what it means to teach, to learn, and to be an adult.

In recognizing the colonized child, I also recognize that parents, educators and administrators are not to blame for this situation. The system that creates the colonized child is an expression of a colonizing mindset that exists across the entire culture within which that child exists. I wish to call it what it is, and to allow for acknowledgement of the predicament in which we find ourselves—a necessary breathing space that may, in time, give way to a new

---

[13]Smith, 2003, p. 2

regard for children in their natural, indigenous state. In turn, this could feed efforts to educate children in a way that allows their native brilliance and individuality to be cultivated within a safe and nurturing educational system. The impact on our culture as a whole would be to increase our celebration of difference within ourselves and in others, unleash collaborative creative problem-solving, and expand our collective imagination of what kind of world we want to live in.

Students are indoctrinated into a passive, receiving, empty vessel model very early in their educational experience. Once this occurs, teachers who try to engage them often face students who seem unable to see themselves in any other way. In an interview with an award-winning public high school teacher, I encountered frustration over the lack of motivation and inspiration in his/her students:

> Well, getting kids to write papers where they don't plagiarize or rely exclusively on Wikipedia is one of the challenges of modern education. I was so naïve and foolish when I started teaching ten years ago that my view toward my students was that we were colleagues in the learning process. They would try and I would try and we would sort of reach a mutual knowledge understanding, and that's just bullshit. You know what I mean? Because first of all…they're inculcated into a very passive model, and even when I tell them to take notes, they won't, so does it get more passive? They are physically there, so I guess I should be happy they walked through the door and sat down, but that's all

they're doing…they're taking up oxygen! That gets very tiring to me as a teacher.[14]

The kind of connectivity and attachment between educator and students (and between educators and administrators) that provides truly fertile ground for learning is precluded by the hegemony. Children learn early on that giving the right answer to a question is the way to obtain rewards and positive reinforcement. They learn that challenging authority will have the opposite effect. When they are seen as vessels to be filled, they come to see themselves in this same way. As social philosopher Hannah Arendt astutely stated, "The aim of totalitarian education has never been to instill convictions but to destroy the capacity to form any." [15]

THE DAMAGE DONE

When punitive discipline is used to enforce rules, children become driven by fear of punishment, lowering their intelligence and capacity, and ultimately losing touch with their intrinsic, inborn motivation to learn and develop. This entire dynamic can stifle a child's naturally imaginative, curious way of exploring the world—her indigenous wisdom, expressed over time. She learns to conform, behave, and achieve according to the expectation that she is no more than a machine who can be controlled, or is in constant trouble for failing to do so. From a very early age, most children become compliant recipients of something

---

[14]Larry, personal communication, August 11, 2007
[15]Hannah Arendt, 1968, p. 168

that passes for knowledge, but that amounts to little more than memorizing data that are rapidly forgotten.

The colonial educational mindset runs counter to what is known about beneficial child attachment and the importance of the moral elevation of being witnessed, treated with kindness, warmth, and love. Consciousness cannot be manipulated; mindfulness and social-emotional learning in education addresses the need for children to feel safely held in a container of trust, mutual respect, regard, and mutuality. Its absence leaves the feeling self, soul, and love out of a picture where all are required.

Our children are living in a world that is not simply oblivious to their needs, but is actually damaging them. There is mounting research documenting how our current narrow version of success is exhausting the resources of a small group of highly academically talented students through increasing AP requirements and toxic stress of college entrance. And those are the success stories. Far worse is the diminishing potential, sense of overwhelm, and defeat of a far larger group of students. Our failure to act, to demand change both from our institutions and from ourselves, is inexcusable. Either we will continue to show a lack of courage, or we will become proactive and decide that our children deserve schools that develop confident, passionate and happy human beings. Classrooms can be places that cultivate a joy of learning, nurture the mind, body and spirit, and protect our kids from the excesses of a culture defined by materialism.

Perhaps the reason that adult society has been unable to identify and halt the damage being done by the school system is due to the Othering they experienced as children.

Now that they are no longer in the oppressive state, they have no urgency or drive to make a change, since they have presumably peacefully slid into the adult world thanks to their training in school, or merely by aging into adulthood. They have been effectively colonized, socialized to believe this is just the way it should be. When populations of children have their creative freedom curtailed, there is not only a loss to the individual, but the potential for humankind is slowly reduced. Modern dance pioneer Martha Graham said:

> There is a vitality, a life force, an energy, a quickening, that is translated through you into action, and because there is only one of you in all time, this expression is unique.... You are unique, and if that is not fulfilled, then something has been lost. [16]

When individual expression is tamped down by an oppressive system, much can be lost that results in both individual and collective suffering. If a reduction in creative freedom occurs, we as individuals, and society as a whole, cease to grow, and fall short of actualizing our full and holistic capacity.

---

[16]Martha Graham, as cited in Horosko, 2002, p. 92

An Education System in Denial

Western society's response to children who feel increasingly stressed, traumatized and unable to align with an oppressive system—and who act out in response—has resulted in all-time high levels of psychiatric diagnoses and medication of children. Although some children in the United States, and specifically in the Southern California public school system that I researched, have privileges far beyond what our ancestors could even have dreamed, they are not faring as well as their less-privileged counterparts in other nations in some very important ways. The pressure to perform and succeed continues to creep toward hyper-achieving, overscheduled and dehumanizing workloads, leaving youngsters sick, stressed and burned out. For those children who are already traumatized due to poverty and other factors that create ongoing fear and insecurity, behavioral issues and dropping out are common. We are witnessing an epidemic of despair incubated in schools that teach us to live out of connection to ourselves.

Findings from the National Survey of Children Exposure to Violence revealed that in 2014, over one-third of children ages seventeen and under were exposed to violence at least once, either as a victim or witness, in that year alone. One-in-ten reported experiencing a physical assault-related injury and one-in-twenty girls reported experiencing sexual assault or abuse.[17] Prevalence of suicide among youth is alarming. According to the Centers for Disease Control and Prevention, suicide is the third leading cause of death among children ages ten to fourteen, and the second leading cause of people between the ages of fifteen and thirty-four.[18]

School violence, including bullying and physical assault, is also at record levels. According to the Centers for Disease Control and Prevention, in data collected in 2015 among students grades nine to twelve, they found that "7.8 percent reported being in a physical fight, 5.8 percent reported that they did not go to school on one or more days in the previous thirty days because they felt unsafe at school or on their way to or from school; 4.1 percent reported carrying a weapon (gun, knife, or club on school property on one or more days in the thirty days before the survey; 6 percent reported being threatened or injured with a weapon on school property one or more times in the previous twelve months; and 20.2 percent reported being bullied on school property while 15.5 percent reported being bullied electronically during the previous twelve months."[19]

Trauma in children can go easily unnoticed simply because those who make up the school system are not aware,

---

[17] Finkelhor, Turner, Shattuck, & Hamby, 2015
[18] National Institute of Mental Health, 2017
[19] Centers for Disease Control and Prevention, 2016

or perhaps they are not trained to recognize and respond to those experiencing trauma, and thus they cannot provide the resources to meet the needs of their students. Rather than wondering what is wrong with the student and making assumptions, dismissing their behavior, or trying to fix them by teaching them how to be like us and grow up as an acceptable citizen, we ought to ask what happened to this child to cause this type of behavior.

The incidence of youth diagnosed with a mental health disorder is increasing. In 2007, a study of over 70,000 American youth aged seven to eighteen found that 7.8 percent had been given an ADHD diagnosis and 4.3 percent took ADHD medications. [20] This comprises more than 2 million American children: at least one per every classroom of twenty-five to thirty children. A growing number of young people have been on medication longer than off it. Findings from another study that collected parent-reported data in 2011-13 revealed 9.5 percent of children and adolescents aged six to eleven and 11.8 for those aged twelve to seventeen, respectively[21] In a more recent study in 2016, results from interviewing parents revealed that 9.6 percent of children aged six to eleven and 13.6 percent of adolescents aged twelve to seventeen were diagnosed with ADHD.[22] In 2009, 2 million youth (8.1 percent of those aged twelve to seventeen) reported major depressive episodes over the past year; youth with depressive episodes were roughly twice as likely to smoke, use illicit drugs, and drink alcohol. According to varying definitions of the disorders, between 1 percent and 4

---

[20] Visser, Lesesne, & Perou, 2007
[21] Pastor et al., 2015
[22] National Resource Center on ADHD, n.d.

percent of youth nine to seventeen years old have been diagnosed with Conduct Disorder/Disruptive Behavior Disorder and/or Oppositional Defiant Disorder, impacting 1 percent to 6 percent of the school-age population. According to the National Youth Risk Behavior Survey, over a twelve-month span, 6.5 percent of ten to twenty-four-year-olds had attempted suicide; 14.5 percent had seriously considered it.[23]

In addition to ADHD, major depression and anxiety are increasingly common mental disorders that can be seen in children and adolescents. For example, in 2016, major depression was shown to affect 12.8 percent of adolescents aged twelve to seventeen, which is a 4.7 percent increase of 2009. Moreover, research has found the onset of anxiety to emerge before age twelve.[24]

This drastic increase in diagnoses and a concomitant rise in the medicating of children should send a significant message to those with the power to change the system that these children are railing against and underachieving within. Instead of recognizing that these children need developmental help, appropriate rites of passage, and in some cases skilled psychotherapeutic guidance that provides relationship and connection, we medicate them into submission and perpetuate the system that may be contributing to their suffering. Rather than being seen as a canary in a coal mine—suggestive of a poisonous system—we see the child as the problem.

The oppressed, at-risk child then may enter adulthood with distinct handicaps regarding emotional, creative,

---

[23] Eaton et al., 2007
[24] Beesdo, Knappe, & Pine, 2009

and relational intelligence, as well as lacking traditionally valued survival skills of intuition and problem-solving. Additionally, by removing the arts and physical education, colonizing reduces to pathology the essential tendencies of childhood: enchantment, magical thinking, and a deep connection to nature, all of which are psychologically and biologically inherent in the human psyche and manifested from very early childhood. What if the educational mainstream were to embrace the indigenous qualities of the child as crucial aspects of their education, as some alternative models do? This question might not be worth asking if our public schools were successful, but they are not. Learning, as educator and feminist theorist bell hooks framed it, is "not merely to share information but to share in the intellectual and spiritual growth of our students."[25] The goals of the American educational system have become focused on "producing a very predictable outcome and being able to measure that outcome compared to other schools and other kids in the country, and between countries."[26] Having become hooked on data, we have lost sight of the basic goal of nurturing children toward being loving, humane and creative adults.

An educational system not founded in love and a reverence for soul can yield learners who feel unseen, unheard, and unsafe. When there is no place for the feeling self to participate in the learning process, little true learning takes place. In order to honor the separation of church and state, all aspects of children's spirituality and development of emotional self have been removed from the public school system. In order to avoid religious controversy, classrooms

---

[25] bell hooks, 1994, p. 13
[26] Dan Williams, personal communication, August 13, 2007

have become spiritually empty. Liberals have been sued for teaching New Age practices, and Christians fear that secularists will resist efforts to provide spiritual guidance in the classroom. Many religious groups aren't even included in the conversation. Collectively, we have reached a standoff, and our children have been the losers.[27]

Additional concerns have been raised by critics of affective education that addressing issues of spirit, self-esteem, self-actualization, or mindfulness is tantamount to practicing psychotherapy or hypnotism, or is simply a waste of academic time. Essential qualities of being positive contributors to our society are deemed soft and not valuable. One news story in May 2013 addressed a lawsuit brought by several parents against a San Diego school district that tried to start a non-religious yoga program for its students; they claimed that the children were being indoctrinated into a set of spiritual teachings. In an article about a highly successful mindfulness and social-emotional learning program called MindUP, *Scientific American* writer Ingrid Wickelgren stated:

> MindUP can interfere with a child's innate self-regulator, the conscience, impeding his moral development and thus his ability to learn. Rather than help him develop self-control, it trains him to manipulate his mind and manipulate others to get pleasurable feelings for himself... Mindfulness meditation such as this can be a way of bringing the mind into an altered state of consciousness. Many people who practice meditation have encountered unexpected negative side effects such as a sensation of being

---

[27] Kessler, 2000, p. 12

disconnected from one's body or from reality, among other frightening reactions. [28]

From another point of view, depth psychology seeks to elucidate the integrated nature of inner and outer life. It holds that any division between these parts of the self is manufactured; therefore, attempts to educate them separately or, as is the case in most educational institutions, to educate the academic/intellectual self while ignoring or actively suppressing the other aspects of self, have led to our current predicament. Thus, we may have unknowingly designed an educational system lacking in soul and absent the power of love and connection.

Love and the Soul in Education

Soul describes the non-corporeal essence of a human being; the parts of the self that make feeling, thought, and conscious action possible. Futurist Robert Sardello defined soul as an "imaginative possibility," having three distinct qualities. First, it is motivated toward the future. Second, it must be regarded as existing within the conscious self. Third, soul is not restricted to the human conscious—it is also external and is found in the world beyond individuals. [29]

Love is the very essence of soul. It is the force that inspires connected relationship and the energy that moves between people—and the entire natural world itself—when positive regard and mutual respect exist. Love is the positive energy that all living things are drawn

---

[28] Wickelgren, 2012
[29] Sardello, 1996

toward and through which all living things grow. Love is directed toward developing the individual in order to create an exchange between self and other. Further, love is directed toward consciousness. Love, too, comes out of empathy, which often emerges from trauma and grief. We must teach our children that grieving can be viewed as an awakening of soul consciousness, able to give us the gift of experiencing from another's perspective. Love desires most of all to be related to the world in its fullness, its grieving as well as its joy.

I believe love is needed to both re-imagine the child's educational experience and to understand the nature of the child's psyche as a universal, although often subverted, way of being that does not need to be colonized or civilized, but rather to be witnessed, cultivated and enhanced, as well as guided and informed. Being directed toward that which draws the child's curiosity provides feelings of potential and aligns soul with ego, that is, a well-developed ego. Approaching the child from this perspective has tremendous impact. It implies an active knowing that the individual is part of something larger—the soul of the world enacted through each of us and realized in relationship. Especially when a child's unique genius proves difficult to see outside of our current way of doing things, love can lead the way if we are willing to follow it. How would schooling look if love and soul were our guiding forces in that realm? Adopting love as our leading motive in education will require immense courage. Education activist Parker Palmer describes teaching as the creation of:

> ...a space in which the community of truth is practiced...The hallmark of the community

of truth is in its claim that reality is a web of communal relationships, we can know reality only by being in community with it.[30]

The bonus to this way of educating our children is that we adults are liberated right along with them, since a liberatory mindset cannot tolerate oppression of anyone.

The Securely Attached Student

Attachment is a process whereby safe and trusting relationships are formed between caregiver and child, enabling children to take risks, risk failure, and be resilient. While primary attachment relationships occur between parents and children, teachers are important secondary attachment figures. One way in which an emphasis on love in education would shift the colonizing mindset is through the fostering of securely attached relationships between teachers and students. Because we send our children to school before they have fully developed a secure attachment to their parents/caregivers, teachers naturally become substitute attachment figures, and it is through this attachment that children are inspired to learn, stretch, and endure challenges.[31]

Attachment to a teacher provides a secure harbor for the child and a sense of purpose and love in the teacher, encouraging the maintenance of a responsive relationship that serves the needs of both. Securely attached caregivers respond to children not out of an abstract notion of that child's needs or what might be for his own good, but out of

---

[30] Parker Palmer, 1998, p. 95
[31] Riley, 2011

43

an empathic bond. This bond creates great sensitivity on the part of the teacher: Not only does she know, intuitively, when the child needs a refuge and time/space to step back from challenges, but also when it makes the most sense to allow the child to stretch, try, and possibly fail at something—a response psychologist Winnicott referenced as "empathically failing the child."[32] The current hegemony discourages the formation of the loving, empathic bond that makes this possible.

In a securely attached relationship with a teacher, a child feels safe to explore; a child who is insecurely attached to primary caregivers has special need of a corrective version of this relationship in school.[33] If this does not happen, that child's urge to explore, play, and learn will be reduced. Students must feel safe enough to take risks in order to succeed in life. No punitive model, no system of extrinsic rewards, and no government program to pressure schools to squeeze academic success out of their students can achieve what this loving attachment can.

Grounding an educational paradigm in love means grounding it in a caring, securely attached relationship of self to other, of self to world, and of individual learners to themselves and to learning. Put more simply, education at its best is grounded in loving relationships. Children don't discover their own identity in isolation; rather it is negotiated through connection and dialogue, partly overt, partly internal, with others. My identity crucially depends on my dialogical relations with others...in the culture of authenticity, relationships are seen as the key loci of

---

[32] Winnicott, 2002, p. 14
[33] Riley, 2011

self-discovery and self-affirmation.[34] Because identity is created within relationship rather than in isolation, the more formal, distanced model of teacher/student that is encouraged in the public system creates a less than fully free and safe environment for children to grow as learners.

If soul is directed toward and by the future, the question of there being soul in the classroom must be posed. Does colonizing the child's imagination create a split between a developing sense of culture and self by diminishing and reducing to pathology the essential tendencies of childhood? An educational system that supports the development of the child's imagination and soul—that refuses to treat this as a land to be invaded and transformed into a place where reason and objective facts take priority—gives birth to various benefits (i.e., social and emotional intelligence) for the individual and ultimately for the community.

Approaching the child from this perspective suggests that the development of wholeness, or in Jung's term, individuation, begins not at midlife, but at the start of and throughout childhood. The child learns that to be an individual does not mean living in unique solitude, detached from the world in self-centeredness, keeping self, soul, and heart artificially separate from her education. Rather, it implies an active knowing that the individual is a part of something larger: the soul of the world. It is through such a depth psychological lens that we can illustrate how the child's psyche can be approached and tended in a way that engages a global community based on empathy, compassion, and consciousness.

---

[34] Taylor et al., 1994, p. 34

Although many other factors come into play in the poor performance of America's schools, including the powerful impact of socioeconomic inequality, I maintain that the failure of the current educational model is connected to the general nature of interaction between adults as colonizers and children the colonized, whose natural innate wisdom goes ignored or is actively stifled in the educational process. Colonizing forces can only carry out their oppressive agendas when the feeling function goes unchecked, and if this is so, it constitutes a fundamental ideological error in the way we teach our children. Until this is addressed, as it has been in a handful of schools, no change in the way academics are taught or schools are held to account will change the course for children who are suffering. As happens with any system built on a fundamental ideological error—which gives rise to a bad set of assumptions and beliefs about what we are doing, why we are doing it, and how it should be done—it becomes impossible to begin to make better choices without reconsidering that initial ideological error. Only when we have done that can we move forward into a more effective ideology and paradigms that mirror it.

ALTERNATIVES TO THE COLONIZED CHILD

WHEN VIEWED WITHIN the theoretical frame of liberation psychology and through the lens of depth psychology, the majority of modern classrooms appear to have an oppressive impact on children. This oppression impacts children at the levels of attachment, development of emotional and social skills, and concept of self, reducing children's ability to learn effectively and creating harm at the level of the individual's sense of subjective agency and value. It deprives children of their natural and innate wisdom and the natural flowering of their own unique gifts. In some instances, it makes gestures that appear to give students some level of choice in the classroom, but in my conversations both within and beyond my initial research, these so-called student-centered gestures generally turned out to be meaningless. What was being called student-centered learning was more about the students *feeling* they have the ability or power to co-create the classroom culture than about students actually doing that.

A thorough examination of the broader, societal impact of this oppressive system was beyond the scope of my inquiry. Yet, there is no self outside of world, and so where soul is lacking in education of the individual, that lack is projected into the world. As I learned in the study of depth psychology, our understanding of soul must free itself from the limiting confinement to individual life alone, and develop the capacity to feel itself in everything in the outer world—my soul as part of world soul. What impacts the individual impacts the world. What deprives the individual soul of its utmost expression deprives the world of its most loving manifestation.

One must also consider the impact of the educational experience on children's overall health and well-being. In public health research, health care was not what created health in a population; an entity called social capital appeared to have a much stronger impact.[35] Social capital is generated through sharing, caring, mutuality, a level playing field socioeconomically, and a sense of safety, trust, and interrelatedness for individuals within community.[36] Only a child's experiences with her own family in infancy and early childhood are more important forces in the generation of a child's social capital—and by association, present and future health—than his or her experience in the educational system. While most experts in this area believe that greater socioeconomic equality will turn the tide of diminishing social capital, it is also prudent to address ways in which social capital can be actively built in schools. Providing mutuality, social-emotional learning, and love in education are a good start.

[35] Hawe & Shiell, 2000
[36] Putnam, 2010

Some children are able to manage typical schooling well and go on to become successful students and individuated adults, but many carry invisible limits to a full expression of their creative potential. On a larger scale, it appears that the American educational system is in trouble, and that schooling is not fulfilling a function true to its highest purpose: to facilitate each individual's vitality and gifts into their most worthy offerings, while helping them to become loving, caring, purposeful participants in the life of the world.

Writing way back in 1914, outspoken educator H.T. Musselman presciently saw a devolution in the role of play as a natural teacher. He bemoaned the transformation of schooling into something regimented, tedious, and working against the child's natural impulse to curiosity and participation in her environment.

> In this rapidly moving, utilitarian age, our educational systems are swept along in the hurrying stream of man's restlessness. We are overanxious to advance children's education rapidly; we begrudge the time it takes to develop normally and naturally. We have not understood or appreciated the meaning and value of play.[37]

Even then, he saw the propensity to regard play only as a means of expending superfluous energy; a safety-valve, as it were, for pent-up steam; as amusement or recreation only. While play is all of these, it serves a much greater purpose in the child. It is a tremendous power that fuels the

---

[37] Musselman, 1914, p. 27

advancement of the educational trinity—physical, mental, and moral development. In earliest childhood, work and play are one, physical activity is spontaneous, driven by curiosity and joy. Something is wrong when education becomes an unpleasant task that requires reward and punishment, a kind of drudgery, a thing from which to escape. Because of the failure to maintain the natural balance between mental, emotional and physical activity, it often results in the physical deterioration of those who reach the highest levels of education. In a schooling system that understands the value of play, the value of imagination in the classroom where students are so engaged, emphasis would shift from standardized correctness and directed toward liberation, allowing for the natural and creative use of information and language.

The importance of not just love, but unconditional love, in creating productive relationships is boiled down to simple terms: Unconditional love is the bedrock of resilience because it creates security.[38] Specifically, love is never withdrawn or threatened to be withheld based on a behavior, but rather is based on the child's humanity and therefore is non-negotiable. If the oppressive nature of standard schooling is to be transformed, and focus is placed on a way of teaching and learning that integrates love, soul, mutuality, the power of the feeling self, and the depth of the indigenous, we can look to the world of alternative schooling for guidance.

---

[38] Ginsburg & Jablow, 2011, p. 22

EDUCATING THE INDIGENOUS CHILD

Traditionally, public schools in the West have neither considered developing nor emphasizing the innate and earthly-connected aspects children are born with. In fact, senses and sensibilities that remind us of our kinship with animal, plant, and stone wisdom, and contact with our ancestors through dreams, ritual and visions, are thought to be nonsense and are totally negated. Against the backdrop of a purely scientific, rational and data-dominated field, children who retain such contact with the unseen and unheard world can be viewed more like indigenous people.

People who have not been exposed to the so-called civilizing processes of the West have maintained access to modes of perception and sensing capabilities that keep them in a flow of intelligible communication with the non-human as well as the human world. People in highly industrialized regions have allowed these innate capacities to atrophy. The result is an overvaluing of human reason and domination and forgetting the delicate interdependence of the earth community. This has effected a tragic loss of health, balance, and harmony—ecologically, emotionally, and spiritually.

What would happen if we deliberately cultivated the indigenous knowing and being of children? Could changing the educational system be a key in reawakening these innate capacities and putting them back into the life of the world? In her exploration of indigenous sensibilities, psychologist Tayria Ward discovered:

> ...that the ways in which Westerners have regarded and treated indigenous peoples the world over—the unapologetic conquest, disrespect, violence, oppression, and marginalization—are exactly how we have tacitly been trained to treat the indigenous aspects of our own natures.[39]

The rejection of the elemental, instinctual selves of indigenous people, and the subsequent damage such disregard and mistreatment have done to their psychic and emotional well-being, makes it clear we must pay attention to how we may be harming our children. When we consider our own inner child to have possessed this original knowing, it becomes even more clear the power education has to either enhance or erase our connection to the earth and to ourselves.

I am calling for a radical rehumanization of our system of education by welcoming back our feeling selves through the immediacy of self-reflection, self-care, and a practice of love in the classroom. Educator G.H. Smith stated:

> The counter strategy to hegemony is that indigenous people need to critically "conscientize" themselves about their needs, aspirations, and preferences. This calls for a "freeing-up" of the indigenous imagination and thinking, given that one of the important elements of colonization is the diminishment of the indigenous ability to actually imagine freedom or a utopian vision free of the oppressor. Thus a critical element in the "revolution" has to be the struggle for our minds—the freeing of

---

[39] Ward, 2003, p. 7

the indigenous mind from the grip of dominant hegemony. [40]

Children know and may protest when their freedoms are curtailed, but they lack the voice and power to counter such influence. Thus, it is the responsibility of adults to recognize our own oppression, and to work with children to recreate the educational system in a manner that will "conscientize" the culture in which we bring up our children. This term was originally coined in Latin America and describes the effort of making others aware of social and political conditions embedded in a system, especially as a precursor to challenging inequalities of treatment or opportunity.

OTHER MODELS OF EDUCATING

In the spirit of acknowledging that each of us comes into this life with an intelligence that, as transpersonal psychologist Stan Grof said, is "nothing other than your own being… it is a matter of learning how to be awake at more and more levels of "your" own being or Being itself."[41] This way of being involves ways of thinking and being present in the world that are not even remotely suggested within the predominant educational paradigm. It is the responsibility of adults not only to recognize and honor the indigenous aspect in themselves—remembering what is important and true—but also to become open and motivated to recreating the educational system in ways that honor the indigenous wisdom born into every child.

---

[40] Smith, 2003, p. 2
[41] Stan Grof, as cited in Ward, 2003, p. 212

Humanistic education is a holistic form of child education that takes into account all parts of the self (emotional, physical, spiritual) and is based on love and acceptance. Educating the whole child acknowledges multiple aspects of each child's experience, innate gifts and preferences, and integrates them into the educational process. Herein, whole-child education is also referenced as humanistic or liberatory education. The indigenous child is considered as having inherent, naturally existing skills, intelligence, and knowledge that are meant to develop into and through adulthood. Such a child is born curious and has an innate desire to learn through play and interaction with the world. Nature is the child's habitat and it knows itself to be related to the whole of life. A liberatory education is a process of allowing the indigenous wisdom of the child to become an active part of the educational process. This integration is enabled through loving, connected relationship between teachers and students, and in peer relationship between students. There are well-known liberatory programs that practice such values, and I will briefly discuss a few examples, as well as the model my study participants attended.

MONTESSORI

A popular example of liberatory education is the Montessori program, which considers the child to be a partner in his own education from infancy forward. This style of education dictates that "[t]he child is endowed with unknown powers, which can guide us to a radiant future. If what we really want is a new world, then education must take as its aim the development of these hidden possibilities."[42] In the same way men have dominated the earth without an awareness of the wealth that lies within its wholeness, modern man has sought a form of progress through civilization without noticing the treasures that lie hidden in the psychic world of the child. Dr. Maria Montessori believed the sensitive child observes and absorbs language and learning from his environment, which literally form part of his soul and enable him to adapt to life. This, she believed was due to an unconscious power that only exists in childhood.

Pre-empting this power in the early years disrupts the child's individuation and gives the child a sense of something being terribly wrong, driving acting-out behaviors, or a suppression of instinctive curiosity and love of learning. Montessori described the natural urge of the child to learn as "like that of the first tribesmen to wander over the earth." She felt that the instinct to move from one discovery to the next is a natural part of their nature, and it must also form a part of their education. Oppression, she felt, worked against the natural wisdom and discipline, which are just waiting to be awakened in the child. She called upon schools to give the child's spirit space and opportunity for expansion. At the same time, the teacher must remember that [the child's] habitual reactions of defense...are obstacles to the unfolding of his spiritual life and from these the child will have to free himself...[and] this is the starting point of education.[43]

The Montessori method embraces love as a crux of the educational relationship between teacher and child

---

[42] Montessori, 1949
[43] Montessori, 1989, p. 264

and between the child and him or herself. It is seen as an equalizing force between adults and children, bonding them as one in the educational process and aiding them both in learning and growth. Love is at the essence of the child's understanding of the world, and it is the motivation through which he develops his values and full potential. In order to become great, Montessori believed, the grownup must become humble and learn from the child.

Montessori education encourages students to learn from mistakes, and in doing so, to forge closer relationships with others, both peers and adults. Rather than using mistakes to divide and humiliate children, they can be framed such that finding solutions becomes interesting, and a bond between human beings. The oppressive education model uses humiliation and the new model must use liberation: To tell a child that he is bad or wrong offends and insults their subjective integrity, but does not improve them. Our current public school model, which often poses a right/ wrong, true/false answer to many questions, produces an inferiority complex and artificially lowers the personal power and sense of discovery of the child. The new education has the opportunity to be a revolution without violence. Montessori felt that education was *the* non-violent revolution where, if it triumphs, violent revolution will become forever impossible.

Montessori education focuses on connecting with the child at the child's level, without a sense of patronization (colonization) or dismissal based on the perceived ignorance of the child. As educators, we must create an environment appropriate to the developmental needs of the child in order to facilitate learning.

WALDORF

Another alternative form of education allied with an indigenous, affective, mutualistic, whole-child model is the Steiner method, upon which Waldorf schooling is based. The practices of this method are in relation to the specific stages of child development. Rudolf Steiner was a world-renowned artist and scientist whose goal for Waldorf education was to encourage individual creative learning by placing a great emphasis on the arts and to incorporate them into every academic discipline. As Steiner described this method: "Waldorf Education is not a pedagogical system but an art—the art of awakening what is actually there within the human being."[44] Children are considered whole persons in body, mind, and spirit, so that as grown men and women they may bring their powers, their own innate and sacred human qualities, to greater fulfillment. It is an education that serves *the freedom of the human spirit*, which is given freely to the world in order to serve the world in which it exists. Through appreciation and compassion, others are not considered objects to move around and navigate against, but to be in relationship and partnership with and move forward together. [45]

I wonder what happened to some of the exciting experimental movements in education that were blossoming in the Sixties, Seventies and Eighties? Outside of select private schools that have been able to maintain alternative models of learning that came out of that time, the humanistic education movement has all but disappeared. The wisdom of combining the psychological,

---

[44] Waldorf Education, n.d.
[45] Pulice, 2010

mental, physical, and emotional aspects of the child in learning environments was an exciting experiment. This book intends to demonstrate a need for these approaches to return as ways to bring love and soul back into an educational system that oppresses students, teachers, and administrators.

CONFLUENT EDUCATION

Confluent Education describes the "integration or flowing together of the affective and cognitive elements in individual and group learning, sometimes called humanistic or psychological education."[46] In this context, Confluent Education is used as a general representation of soul-based, love-based educational approaches.

Developed in the 1960s and 1970s at the University of California, Santa Barbara, Confluent Education's focus rests upon addressing "one crucial polarity in the process of Western civilization that is of directly relevant concern: the dehumanizing versus the humanizing society" [47] as manifested in our educational system. Its aim is to cultivate the potential of each unique human being, allowing that person's potential to reach its summit of possibility. Focus is on the student as a thinking (cognitive) and feeling (affective) being, providing a fertile ground for learning. It is built around a supposition that without allowance for and cultivation of the feeling self, the intellectual self does not truly learn, and that joy, passion, fear, and anger (among other emotions) must all be acknowledged and addressed as part of the living truth of education.

[46] Brown, 1971/1977, p. 1
[47] Brown, 1971/1977, p. xii

No human being can thrive without soul or love and its full expression; leaving these elements out of schooling makes no sense. When schools systematically exclude heart and soul, students become depressed, anxious, attempt suicide, practice self-harm, or develop eating disorders and substance abuse. These students struggle to find the motivation to learn, to stay in school, or to pay attention in class. Straight-A students drive BMWs on their way to shooting fellow students and attempting to incinerate their school with explosives. Welcoming soul into the classroom is not a panacea for all these ills; but it is crucial for addressing the suffering of our youth.[48]

Confluent Education was first conceived as a response to what its creators saw as a growing schism between young people and those they considered "the establishment" [e.g. adults in power].[49] Even then, its founders believed that increasing episodes of violence from young people indicated that the systems in which they were enmeshed were failing; that "a primitive response in a socialized person is often a 'last' response, used when all else has seemed to fail."[50] Now, nearly fifty years later, the divide seems even greater between the system and the young people we call digital natives.

SANTA BARBARA MIDDLE SCHOOL

Santa Barbara Middle School, a private school for grades six through nine, embraces Confluent Education and

---

[48] Kessler, 2000, p. xii
[49] Brown, 1971/1977, p. 6
[50] Brown, 1971/1977, p. 6

intentionally cultivates indigenous education methods. One of its founders described his interest in bringing indigenous education methods into the program, studying ancient cultures that included vision quest, initiatory processes, and what surprised everyone, he claimed, was "that they *worked!* If you looked around the world at ancient cultures, they all took a sense of the sacred as very important. School must refer to a sense of the sacred. We are more than physical and mental beings." At Santa Barbara Middle School, all traditions are honored openly. Most schools don't even want to touch that.[51]

Indigenous methods, the power of myth, the heroic, working with alternative learning styles, forging authentic relations between adults and young people, an educational paradigm founded on love—this is where the tribal past speaks to the needs of the present.

> The newest game in town is the oldest game in town...we found that the tribal speaks. We have an academic component, of course, but that is only a first step, not the only step, and it is no more important than creativity, community, global, friendships, and mastering our own limitations.[52]

This indigenous approach is also a depth psychological approach. The parallels run deep, and there is a natural affinity when working with children to include indigenous methods of ritual and learning that connect them with the larger earth community.

---

[51] Kent Ferguson, personal communication, 2013
[52] Kent Ferguson, personal communication, 2013

Oppressive systems refute the sentience of the human beings trapped within them. Where colonizers are able to blindly limit, misuse, and devastate the colonized, they must deny that those others are sentient beings with authentic feelings, wants, souls, and loves. Empathic attunement and subjugation/repression are mutually exclusive. When children in such traditional schooling situations react with violence, as they have increasingly since Brown's 1971 prophetic statements, they are doing so because they are stuck in a process that they intuitively recognize will impede their full expression and freedom. Without tools or power to create change, disempowered human beings will either rebel or collapse and give up.

Educator and advocate of critical pedagogy Paulo Freire described the oppressed/colonized individual as having been indoctrinated to see herself as an object instead of as a subject. She is not a do-er, but is done to. She is not filled with her own knowing, but a vessel to be filled, a factory product to be turned out according to specifications handed down from higher up. The educator-as-oppressor projects an absolute ignorance onto others, a characteristic of the ideology of oppression, negates education and knowledge as processes of inquiry. The teacher presents himself to his students as their necessary opposite; by considering their ignorance absolute, he justifies his own existence.[53] The action available to students in this scenario is to receive deposits of information, memorize them, and repeat them back to the teacher, or as students I interviewed called it, "memorize, barf back, and forget." As Freire stated, students have the opportunity to become collectors or

---

[53] Freire, 1970/2005, p. 72

cataloguers of the things they store [54] but ultimately they are never given the opportunity for creativity, transformation, and knowledge.

But rather than rising against it, this educator remains as much a product of oppression as the children upon whom she perpetuates the strict authoritarian discipline of learning equated with suffering. Therefore, when Freire pointed out that the oppressed must become the liberators not only of themselves, but of their oppressors as well, he was calling attention to this: the child and educator, as well as the parent/caregiver, cannot be separated through an I-It perspective, also known as Othering.[55] In my research, I found teacher burnout to be linked to the dehumanizing climate and oppressive factory-like productivity model being applied to the human beings they are there to help and to love. It is clear that each of us must take up the task of self-liberation so that we may be more able to assist future generations in their full expression.

The U.S. Department of Education's[56] stated goals say nothing about educating the whole child. Its list of goals for primary and secondary school education include generalities such as "prepare all students for college and career," "demonstrate progress in turning around low-performing schools," and "improve students' ability to afford and complete college."[57] Few would argue that the ultimate stated aim of any system of education is not

---

[54] Freire, 1970/2005, p. 72

[55] Pulice, 2010

[56] U.S. Department of Education, 2012

[57] U.S. Department of Education, Priority Performance Goals, February 2012

addressed with goals like these. What about self-esteem, character, integration of the feeling self, somatic, and social intelligences? Until we recognize the importance of school climate, and the need to define it as inclusive of students' and teachers' well-being, sense of belonging, and emotional safety, our measures of schools will be inadequate. The inclusion of statistics that include the quality of care, connection, community and choice for the human beings who spend their days together will be a step toward rehumanizing the quality of learning.

Including character as part of curriculum, especially during adolescence, creates an educational system that works with children's real developmental interests, which prioritize relationship and novel experiences. A resonance emerges more vividly in adolescent students and certainly has its roots in the earliest years of education. The adolescent slowly begins to be more aware of the effects of actions on others and to be able to inhibit impulsive behaviors. The limbic areas, which are concerned with emotional responses, mature earlier than the frontal lobes, which are concerned with judgment and reasoning. During these years, emotional development outpaces executive control, so an education that recognizes this and meets the child where they are may avoid much of the difficulty experienced in adolescence. [58]

The current educational system is highly focused on facilitating the development of logic and reason, rewarding compliance and following exact directions, accelerating this development far beyond that of the feeling self in order to mold productive and marketable members of

---

[58] Wilkinson, 2006, p. 115

society. This system of education defies the natural order of brain development because it provides no support for or acknowledgement of the adolescent's emerging emotional intelligence capabilities. When the child's developmental interests are not represented in the educational system, they are likely to find it frustrating, oppressive, and unresponsive to their needs, and many give up trying.

The argument in favor of a non-hierarchical, humanistic, whole child-centered educational system is not an argument for reduction of academic standards. If effective, humanistic approaches foster improved school climate and students feel seen, safe, and understood. They are more inclined to take agency in their own educations. They come to *want* to perform better, and this is what improves academic performance. Studies have borne this out. A 2013 study funded by the California Department of Education involved forty schools that performed better than expected based on the socioeconomic status of their students. [59] The researchers suspected that school climate might be a factor. The study confirmed this hypothesis: that these "beating the odds" schools scored much higher on a survey that measures school climate (average: 82nd percentile) compared with struggling schools that did only as well as expected based on their demographics (average: 49th percentile). Other investigations confirmed a link between greater social/emotional competence and academic success.[60]

---

[59] Voight, Austin, & Hanson, 2013
[60] Parker et al., 2004

SOCIAL-EMOTIONAL LEARNING-AHA!

An example of a social-emotional learning (SEL) program is the non-profit AHA!. Its role since the organization's founding in 1999, as a response to the Columbine shootings, has been to work both in schools and in an after-school program to fill the gap between schools' academic, achievement focus and the real needs of adolescents for emotional support, character guidance, and social-emotional education. AHA! is a place where teens can get to know themselves more deeply and reflect upon things that matter most to them with skilled adult facilitators serving as mentors and guides. While AHA! is a valuable program, it is attempting to fill a huge need that may not exist if its curriculum, and others like it, could be made a part of what public schools naturally do to address the full humanity of our youth.

Schools like Montessori, Waldorf, and Santa Barbara Middle School treat children as vessels full of their own particular wisdom and knowing. Mainstream public education predominantly treats children as empty vessels to be filled or as savages in the language of discourse, waiting to be colonized and improved. This became starkly apparent in my research, which included an initial survey and a follow-up in-depth interview process with young people who were exposed to both.

Having directly experienced both models, the interview participants had unique insight: they knew how it felt to be educated in a "whole-child" system and to pass from there into a more narrowly focused, test-based, quantitatively evaluated hierarchical model. I found the classroom to be an environment of either marginalization (Othering) or integration (wholeness)—a place where the essential nature of the child is either met within the classroom and an exchange of soul and spirit are welcome, or not. Using both a critical and appreciative approach, I sought to find the causes behind an apparent sense of alienation and oppression being observed and self-described by teens, while also seeking a rationale and an approach that would not create these impacts on children. Examples of approaches that were experienced as liberatory were compared in the context of individual students, and their impacts were examined via both heuristic and hermeneutic analyses.

Depth and liberation psychologies are concerned with soul, and by proxy, love. Both disciplines may be enhanced by the inclusion of all children as such, regardless of additional demographic qualifiers, a population which may in fact be marginalized. So, too, does education stand to be enhanced by the inclusion of the perspectives of both depth and liberation psychology. Schooling is an area of interest to all, as it is a shared experience crossing all socioeconomic, gender, and racial borders. Jung wrote of the outcome of the individuation process as being a renewed sense of wholeness. Including this psychological view as one desired outcome of the educational process can eventually lead to positive change in the way we educate children.

The current public model of education may be limited to producing reliable consumers and passive participants in the system, leaving the mark of oppression as characterized by a lack of connection to one's self, without a higher sense of purpose or participation in a world they do not create. Holistic education is founded in love and soul.

CURRENT CHALLENGES IN EDUCATION

EDUCATION IS AT ITS ROOTS about developing human capital, so how we define our goals and tend this precious resource, and whether we succeed or fail, has far-reaching impact on society. We cannot improve schools merely by reorganizing their structure and management if we do not first take into account their value and purpose. What is required here is a renewed focus on educational vision. The keys to that focus are not only curriculum and instructional improvement but include improvement in the working conditions of both teachers and students. Importantly, schools cannot be improved without some focus on the needs of children who grow up in poverty. These children start out with a disadvantage, and they need extra time, resources, and attention to catch up with their peers. Inclusion of curriculum in the arts—dance, music, theater, visual arts—in public schooling is even more important for the healing and integration it offers to kids who are challenged. The arts provide a place for soul and the feeling self in school, and their dwindling presence there has been another canary in the coal mine over the past several decades.

If we were to try to narrow reasonable goals for our educational system down to a single word, we might use the term: success. We all want children to succeed. Although there are many ways to define success, we all know it when we see it: a successful person is generally happy, optimistic, and secure, with a life that works well; who has the ability to risk, endure failure and loss, and experience genuine emotion and connected relationships. But in reality, the school system is rigged to create a docile proletariat. Teachers reward repressed robots. Research has proven that the students with the highest GPAs are the ones who score the lowest on measures of creativity and independence, and the highest on measures of punctuality, predictability, and dependability.

The classroom should be a space for developing skills that are used for the development of one's own mental and emotional well-being, and not only for the development of academic skills. Qualities such as empathy, persistence, self-esteem, curiosity, resilience, self-control, and conscientiousness are examples that take into account the whole person, rather than merely focusing on their cognitive skills. Unfortunately, such characteristics have received little focus in the design of modern educational systems. Corporate America's rulers wanted to staff their offices with bland and reliable sheep, so they created a school system that selected for those traits. [61]

Reasons for the failures of modern schooling include overloading the hypothalamic-pituitary-adrenal (HPA)

---

[61] Bowles & Gintis, 1976, Schooling in Capitalist America, p. 72

axis, or the fight-or-flight response in children. We now know that toxic stress levels, especially in infancy and childhood, produce all kinds of serious and long-lasting negative effects—physical, psychological, and neurological.[62] Children who have experienced multiple severe traumas like the death of a family member, having a drug-addicted parent, being placed in foster care, or witnessing a murder have been found to have dramatically higher odds of certain long-term health risks, and increased odds of dropping out of school. But the point is also relevant to describe what occurs when children are stuck in a high pressure, non-nurturing and oppressive system without a voice of their own. The impact of poverty on children is not only poverty itself but the stress of insecurity that compromises children's executive function (defined as the ability to deal with confusing and unpredictable situations and information without acting-out related to emotional impulses).

EFFECTS OF TRAUMA AND STRESS

According to the National Child Stress Network, one out of every four children will be exposed to at least one traumatic event by the time they reach the age of sixteen, affecting learning, health, and behavior. Trauma can be a result of various types of experiences, including neglect, homelessness, violence, being a victim of abuse, bullying, abandonment, and poverty. Trauma in children can go unnoticed simply because those who make up the school system are not aware, are not trained to recognize and

---

[62] Tough, 2012, p. 13

respond to those exhibiting symptoms, and/or remain unable to provide resources to meet the needs of their students.

Toxic stress happens when there is prolonged activation of stress response systems in the absence of protective relationships, and it has been found to have a damaging effect on children's development.[63] When there is no safe adult to respond to and serve as a buffer for the child's sense of overwhelm, their stress response remains activated longer than it should, and actually harms their emotional and physical development. Parts of the brain that are responsible for learning and reasoning suffer a reduction in neural connections as a result of prolonged activation of stress. When a child experiences a traumatic event or prolonged adversity, the body responds by disrupting the development of brain architecture and other organ systems, increasing the risk for stress-related disease and cognitive impairment, well into the adult years.

Children can become more sensitive to stress as a result of trauma, even a single event, making it difficult for them to communicate their needs and respond appropriately to threats to their well-being, both emotional and physical. An ongoing stressor such as abuse or poverty may produce a fight-or-flight response that is misunderstood, creating a pattern of behavior that is negative, such as disruptive behavior, withdrawal, and acting out. Besides triggering out-of-control responses, toxic stress can have adverse effects on a child's academic performance and ability to work at his or her potential, which can become a pattern of demoralization leading to drop out.

---

[63] Harvard University, n.d.

Some students are not only concerned about passing a class or acing a test, but also taking on a parental role with younger siblings or working with a parent to help provide family income. A high school math teacher told me about a student who often fell asleep in class. While at a food truck late one night in a gas station parking lot, she noticed that same student taking food orders while his father cooked. She later learned that the food truck was his family's only means of survival, and that his labor six late nights a week was essential to the family. Adversity is more common than we may imagine, and without knowing what happened to that student, the system may misdiagnose his behavior incorrectly. Poverty, immigration, and other social barriers invisibly increase stress, and that challenges healthy development.

Studies have found that children who have experienced trauma are especially vulnerable to experiencing stress and trauma in the future, and have shown that adversity in childhood can trigger neurobiological events that can alter brain development. For example, one study illustrated that physical disparities that surface in adulthood can be associated with developmental and biological disruptions that take place in childhood. The cumulative exposure to stressful experiences over time can create chemical changes that lead to physical problems such as heart disease, obesity, chronic pulmonary disease, and mental health disorders, including depression, alcoholism, and drug abuse.[64]

---

[64] Shonkoff, Boyce, & McEwen, 2009, p. 2253

TRAUMA-INFORMED CARE

Children spend a large portion of their time at school, placing teachers and site administration in a role of helping and supporting them on a daily basis. This gives teachers and administration the opportunity to provide a safe space for their students that allow them to feel supported, as well as to help them recover from trauma they may have experienced. Creating a space, or revising an already-created space, to be a safe school is not a "quick fix" done with a Band-Aid; rather, it is a process that takes time and commitment from the school community. According to the Substance Abuse and Mental Health Services Administration (SAMHSA), a trauma-informed" system includes the following:

1. Realizes the widespread impact of trauma and understands potential paths for recovery,

2. Recognizes the signs and symptoms of trauma of those involved in the system,

3. Responds to fully integrating knowledge about trauma into policies, procedures, and practices,

4. Seeks to actively resist re-traumatization.

They offer six guiding principles of trauma-informed care for schools to realize, recognize, and respond to their students, families, and staff to prevent re-traumatization:

1. Safety—Throughout the organization, staff and the people they serve feel physically and

psychologically safe; creating predictable routines in the classroom to give students confidence, help them achieve independence, and reduce anxiety. Predictability at the school level creates a sense of safety. Create conditions for calm. Set up practices in the classroom and school that help create a sense of order and calm, reduce chaos, and minimize feelings of being out of control. Praising people publicly, and holding them accountable privately, creates a sense of psychological safety for students and staff. Use restorative approach to discipline, which focuses on repairing harm through inclusive processes that engage all involved.

2. Trustworthiness and transparency— Organizational operations and decisions are conducted with members of those receiving services. Being transparent and including students and staff about how and why decisions are made creates conditions for trust. Relationships are fundamental to this process, and trust is the cornerstone.

3. Peer support and mutual self-help—These are integral to the organizational and service delivery approach and are understood as a key vehicle for building trust, establishing safety, and empowerment. Prioritizing school employee wellness and building a culture that supports collective self-care is essential.

4. Collaboration and mutuality— Collaborations should be highly valued and practiced among administration, staff, and in the classroom. Meaningful and authentic power-sharing strengthens trust and relationships.

5. Empowerment, voice, and choice—Students, families, and all staff must feel empowered, valued, and validated.

6. Cultural, historical, and gender issues—A trauma-informed school actively moves past cultural stereotypes and biases. It recognizes previous history with the system as being a traumatizing experience for many.[65]

ADVERSE CHILDHOOD EXPERIENCES

A measure that many schools have taken to become more aware of their students' level of traumatic experiences is through a scoring system developed by CDC-Kaiser in the late 1990's. They found that the existence of eight adverse childhood experiences (ACEs) among children from birth to age seventeen had a significant impact on long-term health and well-being. Stressors include the following:

Lived with a parent or guardian who got divorced or separated,

Lived with a parent or guardian who died,

Lived with a parent or guardian who served time in jail or prison,

Lived with anyone who was mentally ill or suicidal, or severely depressed for more than a couple of weeks,

Lived with anyone who had a problem with alcohol or drugs,

---

[65] Substance Abuse and Mental Health Services Administration, n.d.

Witnessed a parent, guardian, or other adult in the household behaving violently toward another (e.g., slapping, hitting, kicking, punching, or beating each other up),

Was ever the victim of violence or witnessed any violence in his or her neighborhood,

Experienced economic hardship "somewhat often" or "very often" (i.e., the family found it hard to cover costs of food and housing).[66]

Researchers have found that higher ACE scores are correlated to experiencing academic challenges, as well as negative behavioral and health problems.[67]

THE CHALLENGE OF PRIVILEGE

As I began to recognize the plight of students of modern schools with dynamics similar to what Freire described, it was driven home by my own children's disappointment upon discovering they weren't expected to think critically in public school. As a freshman at the public high school, my daughter was given an assignment to use Kohlberg's stages of moral development to rank the moral stage of a heroine in a Greek myth. Having become used to exercising her own original ideas, as long as she could back them up, she wrote a paper with a novel twist. When she came home with a D on her paper, I suggested she ask to rewrite the paper, but this time write the most obvious response, and see if it would change her grade. She dubiously took the

---

[66] Sacks, Murphey, & Moore, 2014, p. 2
[67] Sacks, Murphey, & Moore, 2014, p. 7

challenge, but when she received an A- for her effortless response, she was insulted and deflated by the prospect of four years of compliance, with her teachers having no interest in her critical or original thought. Welcome to public school, I told her. You can either play by the rules and go on to the college of your choice, or try to fight the system and likely lose. She had experienced firsthand how the Middle School's confluent approach takes a co-creative tack, making students co-creators of knowledge being imparted in the classroom. This is one of the qualities Freire had suggested we should look for in an effective and just pedagogy.

A list of characteristics of successful children, whether they have stress or not, includes grit, self-control, zest, social intelligence, gratitude, optimism, curiosity.[68] Today's mainstream schooling does very little to cultivate these qualities in children. The good news is that children's socioeconomic status does not make or break their ability to develop these characteristics.

THE UNIQUENESS OF MILLENNIALS

An apt term for the teens examined in this study is Millennial. It describes the current generation of children, those born on or after the year 2000, who are coming of age in a world dramatically different from their parents'. This is always true of a new generation, but with the advent of highly personal forms of technology that have become part of nearly every facet of daily life, and that are increasingly woven into education, it appears truer here than for any

---

[68] Tough, 2012, p. 13

generation that came before. The changes have been fast and furious as the world has become radically more connected in certain ways and radically less connected in other ways. For the first time in the history of humans, children are showing their parents the new world order, not the other way around. These young people intuitively understand absolutely crucial elements of what is rapidly becoming a perpetually fluid society. They appear to come in with that understanding, and therefore are given the nickname Digital Native. They hold the keys to all our futures in a way children never have before, while still possessing indigenous understandings that link them to their parents and to all of humanity. How do we cultivate both aspects of the Millennial child? This is a question well-served by a depth psychological approach, where we look deeply into personal, universal, and collective aspects of the human being.

However they might be categorized and defined, there is a percentage of children either less than willing or less able to capitulate when it is demanded that they comply with a system that does not make sense to them. Not all are behaviorally difficult or challenging, but most are in possession of understandings, insights, and ways of thinking that adults do not naturally grasp. Perhaps they represent a natural evolution of children who take a stand against—perhaps to eventually transform—an oppressive system on behalf of their fellow Millennials, for the benefit of all. They may be a support for adults who wish to enroll the support of children themselves in enacting transformation. In viewing children who are failing within the existing educational system, psychology has two choices: to see these children as somehow pathological in exponentially increasing numbers, meriting diagnosis, drugging, or rehabilitation; or to see them as "canaries in the coal mine," to ignore at our collective peril. When miners do not heed the canary, they themselves are doomed.

These children need not be medicated, but supported and given a sense of voice and agency in their worlds. Adults would do well to turn to such system busters to find out what they need from their educational system, and from society. Rather than turn the acting-out child into the identified patient, we must look at the whole family system—in this case, the educational system the child is moving within—in order to understand the ways in which she is in disharmony. The child who is angry, rebels against school or who quietly disengages (as I did), or who expresses symptoms of ADHD, oppositional defiant disorder, depression, or anxiety, is sending an important message to the worlds of education and psychology that something crucial is not serving them. Both fields of depth psychology, where patterns of dysfunction and pathology may be noticed in the collective, and sociology not only stand to be enriched by the inclusion of children's education as a valid point of discussion; they also have potential solutions for reducing the impact of the oppressive educational model.

The Student-Teacher Relationship

It is not only the student who must be regarded as sacred, but the teacher as well. Through such relationship, there is a dynamism that is created that helps to foster individuality of thought and action, thus establishing a pattern of response to a normalized marginalization. Many teachers consider the vocation of teaching as a spiritual calling. Of primary importance is connecting the role of the teacher with the importance of love in education, where knowing is connected to loving. Through the positive connection with one's teacher a transmission of understanding happens that cannot be conveyed any other way, in the presence of the beloved other. If the child who enters the educational system does so as a whole and natural, authentic self, then nothing can be gained by assuming he or she is a *tabula rasa*, which must be filled with collections of data, as in Freire's banking model. There must be a degree of truth, which is not a construct, but a relationship. Such a student-teacher relationship honors truth in ourselves, other persons, and the entire universe which, in the words of Martin Buber, is no longer only "It" but thoroughly and profoundly "Thou," depicting a sacred relationship. In the space of learning, classrooms and school campuses, we can return a sense of a spiritual partnership built on reciprocity and mutuality, rather than hierarchy or hegemony. Therefore, we must consider the teacher's perspective; to teach is to create a space in which the "community of truth" is practiced, where reality is seen as a web of communal relationships, and we engage by being in community with it. Further, good teaching requires self-knowledge: it is a secret hidden in plain sight.[69]

Teachers can be seen as operating through three primary lenses: the intellectual, emotional, and spiritual. In the question of why teach, there is a philosophical stance with which each teacher enters the classroom. There are strong feelings that accompany the experience of both teaching and learning, and they include the diverse ways we answer the heart's longing to be connected with the largeness of life.[70] Because the educational experience is, at heart, one of exchange, a more holistic view of the classroom allows for the teacher's experience to be seen and understood, recognizing that the classroom can either serve to enlarge or diminish the exchange between us.

Much has been written about ways to begin or maintain the kind of transformation that would address the needs of the whole child and create greater success for more children coming through that system. One such author is bell hooks, who believes that education can be seen to be an act of deep reverence and respect for the reciprocal exchange between

---

[69] Palmer, 1998, p. 3
[70] Palmer, 1998, p. 5

teacher and student. The learning process is made easier by teachers who believe their work is not just about delivering information, but rather believe it is a sacred task, to share in the intellectual and spiritual growth of our students.[71] This view of teaching and learning would require nothing short of a paradigm shift in our educational system, and one that has the potential to expand us in both obvious and unseen ways. Hooks pointed to the awakening to love as a way there—more precisely, a recognition of love as central to schooling, politics, workplace, and every other place that matters to human beings. But this requires that we let go of our obsession with power and domination in all aspects of human life, where a foundational ethic of love takes precedence over material advancement.[72]

Only within a loving relationship can a child feel securely attached. A healthy teacher-student and student-school relationship are essential for building resilience in students—a quality that enables them to face challenges, risk failure, and individuate fully. Children who are well-connected to their schools are more likely to thrive educationally, emotionally, and socially. When they view their school as a safe, protected place and believe that the adults at school care about their well-being, children are more likely to take in knowledge while absorbing the invaluable life lesson that learning is pleasurable and rewarding. The need for the formation of healthy connections between teachers and students is clear as they are valuable allies and may pick up on difficulties that parents might miss, especially social difficulties or learning differences. Separating love and care out of

---

[71] hooks, 1994, p. 3
[72] hooks, 2001, p. 87

school, assuming it is the domain of home and family alone, misses one of the biggest opportunities for loving at a societal level, and an important opportunity to grow more resilient, healthy children.

The importance of secure attachment to initial caregivers for child health, well-being, and ability to learn has been a subject of much study. Teachers' own attachment styles— whether they were securely or insecurely attached in their own childhoods—influence their availability for healthy attachment in their classrooms. Teachers are best able to serve students when they themselves have been adequately served and teachers who feel attached to their students can share much more in the joy of their students' achievement than can non-attached teachers.[73] Acknowledgement of these factors is key to creating classrooms characterized by a positive sense of mutuality.

But fear is pervasive in schools, found in students and teachers alike. Whether it is a student, a colleague, a subject, or a self-critical voice in your head, this fear is felt as an alien otherness. An atmosphere of fear can act as a barrier that hinders us from connection and with experiments with truth, as Parker Palmer called them, and it shuts down the capacity to teach and to learn.

In my interviews with administrators and teachers, I discovered the powerful impact of fear in decision-making at multiple levels, where the school environment may be contaminated by a sense of overall lack of emotional safety. Here are some things they said:

---

[73] Riley, 2011, pp. 33-34

"I, I only know what I've seen. And I've seen those teachers that have issues, that have brought things to our boss, and…life was made a little more difficult around here." (Teacher 74)

"It's gotten better. I'd say that this year, but the last couple years I have felt afraid…umm there's a lot of fear over jobs and there are a lot of people who have been really hammered for the last couple of years. And…I think there's been a lot of distrust…with our administration as far as our staff." (Teacher 42)

"I don't have a good relationship with administrators, I never have, and I suspect I never will because they're not trustworthy first and foremost. And because they do not have the best interests of the students and their faculties in mind." (Teacher 77)

"I feel like the good teachers—or the teachers who were doing their jobs—would get punished. I feel like we always got punished. So if you did your job you had to jump through hoops, and I know where they are going with it. I guess I know why they are making us jump through hoops, but it is just, it is just a little frustrating. And so suddenly we all had to know this book, and we had to read this book, everybody had to know what this book was about. And you had to do the do-nows and you had to do the exiting tickets, even if what I was already doing was working…" (Teacher 79)

It is likely that students feel these teachers' frustrations and act out in the same way as when they sense dysfunction in family systems, whether it is openly discussed or not. Fear reduces intelligence in children in the classroom, producing negative thinking and affecting a child's ability and desire to learn. We must break the habit of fear and negative thinking that leads to poor life outcomes. In a fear-based school environment, education retards rather than facilitates learning by instilling fear, anxiety, tension, avoidance of trying and being wrong, and by imposing shame and embarrassment in front of others. This is a compelling argument for why a sense of safety in school is of the utmost importance in learning for young children.

Alfie Kohn demonstrated how fear serves as a driver of both educational choices and damage done to students within an oppressive system. Results from tests that elicit anxiety in students do not serve those students, nor do they give good information about what the system is able to teach. Some test results may not appropriately represent students' potential, skills, and qualifications. Test anxiety has grown into a subfield of educational psychology, and its prevalence means that the tests producing this reaction are not giving us a good picture of what many students really know and can do. The more a test is made to "count"—in terms of being the basis for promoting or retaining students, college entrance, for funding or closing down schools—the more that anxiety is likely to rise and *the less valid the scores become.* [74]

When applied to the child, critical theory calls into question the importance of consciously building rapport between the child and his or her environment. If the concept of power is perhaps natural to the psyche, it is necessary to regard it as developmentally constructive. In other words, supporting empowerment within the

---

[74] Kohn, 2000, p. 5

child and caretaker or teacher to the extent that one is not dominant over the other (thus stopping the tendency toward oppression of each, while keeping in mind that the child's oppressor is really an oppressed child him or herself) creates an environment where suppression is negated. An empowered child and teacher cannot abide oppression, neither as perpetrator nor as victim.

In the field of psychology, it has been proven that through conscious reflection and attunement from a therapist, patients are capable of gaining previously missed secure attachment. This is good news to educators willing to consider acknowledging the fact that such psychological dimensions exist in the classroom. Individuals who receive this kind of attachment in school may need less repair later on as patients in psychotherapy. The greater the attunement of caregivers, whether at home or in school, the more likely to develop secure attachment in the child.[75] Sure attachment was defined as "sensitivity rather than misattunement, acceptance rather than rejection, cooperation rather than control, and emotional availability rather than remoteness."[76] Increasing knowledge of how the brain and learning are supported point to secure attachment as a baseline necessity biologically, emotionally, and in higher level functioning.

A securely attached child is not a child who has been the center of adults' universes—in other words, Othered as an entity to watch and attend to more or less constantly.[77] The securely attached child has been treated as one end of a continuum of life, integrated as part of the adult-centered

[75] Wallin, 2007, p. 16
[76] Ainsworth, as cited in Wallin, 2007, p. 19
[77] Liedloff, 1975/1977

world and taught by example, within the context of a world not divided into child's and adult's compartments. The securely attached child is more likely to find ease in relationship—to be able to form connected relationships with teachers, peers, and others. This comes in part from having naturally developed the capacity to empathize with those others.

No discussion of the problems with mainstream education would be complete without mention of the work of John Taylor Gatto. A past winner of the Teacher of the Year award, he writes from a teacher's point of view regarding the failure of the American school system. He argues that the across-the-board, national curriculum of the school system teaches young people to be submissive, dependent, and confused about their role in society. In his book, *Dumbing Us Down*, he said there were seven problematic lessons modern schooling teaches children.

> 1. *Confusion.* There is no rhyme, reason, or sequential sense to be made of the order in which subjects or ideas are taught to children. "The logic of the school-mind is that it is better to leave school with a superficial tool kit of jargon derived from economics, sociology, natural science, and so on, than with one of genuine enthusiasm" (p. 3).

> 2. *Class position.* Kids are "numbered" in the classroom, taught to stay in their grade, and learn to "fear the better classes and…have contempt for the dumb classes" (p. 4).

> 3. *Indifference.* Kids are expected and trained to be involved in what is going on at that

moment, but whenever a bell rings, they should be prepared to drop what they are doing and immediately transition into their next task or subject. This teaches them that no work is worth finishing; so why care too deeply about anything (p. 6)?

4. *Emotional dependency.* Children become dependent upon "favors" or earned rights from teachers (raised hand to use the bathroom, speak, or go to the drinking fountains) and also for approval and encouragement (p. 7).

5. *Intellectual dependency.* "Good students wait for the teacher to tell them what to do." This teaches children to wait for others to direct them and teaches them that meaning comes from others. In this paradigm, a successful child has a minimum of resistance and a decent show of enthusiasm. Kids who resist this dynamic are labeled "bad" and may end up diagnosed or medicated (p. 8).

6. *Provisional self-esteem.* Kids are constantly evaluated and judged (report cards). Their opinion of self and success in the classroom is determined by the teacher. This teaches "that a kid's self-respect should depend on expert opinion" (p. 10). The lesson of report cards, grades, and tests is that children should not trust themselves or their parents, but should instead rely on evaluation by certified officials.

7. *One can't hide.* Children are always watched; there are no private spaces and no private time. "Students are encouraged to tattle on each other or even tattle on their own parents" (p.

11). Homework is another method of constant surveillance.[78]

Neuroscience has shown the way human neurology develops in a child exposed to appropriate developmental cues, fostering the ability to empathize. Mirror neurons provide us with the ability to imitate and perceive what is going on in the brains of others. Rather than being wired for self-serving competition, imitation and empathy are actually building blocks of evolutionary processes that enhance social and moral empathy.[79] This shows that we are hard-wired for attunement, care, and relationship, which is how young babies and children learn from birth until they are sent to school. A decision to reduce these qualities in education is against the natural grain of being human.

CHILDREN MOST AT RISK

I became curious about whether certain types of children could be at the greatest risk in the current educational system. The gifted or sensitive child can be more easily oppressed, especially if he or she was reared by parents who have been raised within that paradigm themselves. Parents are also subject to oppression in the educational system, particularly when they are tempted to anchor their self-esteem to their children's academic success.[80] They have inherited the oppressive competition model, and sometimes let it influence their parenting when they

---

[78] Gatto, 2005, pp. 3-11
[79] Iacoboni, 2009, pp. 666-667
[80] Levine, 2012

align their own goals for their children firmly with those of the educational system and when young people start to compare themselves to other kids. These realities can create an atmosphere of fear (rather than love) in the educational environment unless explicitly countered by a school's culture.

Thus, there can be an endless recycling of narcissistic wounding going back to ancestral abuses, where the child is instead treated as a commodity, a resource to be used to the extent of the cultural law. This normalization of oppression is a key concept of liberation psychology. For the cycle to be broken, the child must be seen not as a thing to be owned and utilized, but as an autonomous, reciprocating being in his or her own right.

I agree with Jung, who stressed that "giftedness"[81] is not only found in those students who excel in an obvious way, but also in those who might pose behavioral challenges. Teachers thus need to discern between pathology and giftedness, and it is their response that fosters the type of atmosphere supportive of the child's potential.

---

[81] Jung, 1946/1954, p. 137, [CW 17, ¶ 235]

Understanding Underlying Dynamics

Drawing from the literature further supported the foundational premise of this work: That children in public schools may be treated as Others in need of being colonized, and that despite children's complying with this model from their earliest years, this often-blatant disregard of their innate gifts, indigenous understandings, and natural proclivities may have the effect of traumatizing the child. This rejection of their unique genius, or *daimon*, as James Hillman called it, is a distancing move. The modern adult world constructs a distinct population, viewing our young as children who are separate and not-us. Being seen as a marginalized group that is not yet fully human may thereby prevent the formation of the securely attached, loving relationships that provide a truly safe space for learning, keeping schools from addressing the whole child—mind, soul, and body. Teachers, administrators, and parents are all asked to buy into this same model by a compulsory government school system, and shifting it will require an awareness described in the field of liberation psychology: a clear vision of what damage the current system might be doing, and a vision of the common aims of all who wish to educate children as free thinkers from a position of love and secure relationships above all.

LIBERATION PSYCHOLOGY

Americans have been looking at how our schools' test scores stack up against our international competition for so long, we may be missing what it is actually doing to them. We no longer hear the paradigm-shifting conversations and proposals of the Sixties and Seventies that sought to enhance children's academic and emotional well-being and social consciousness. But with the Civil Rights and Women's Rights movements opening up opportunities in higher education for working class, racial and ethnic minorities, and women, critical theorists began to question the mainstream view of compulsory education as an always-benign, universal good that just needed to be equally available.

Liberation psychology uses a lens that examines the individual and group psychological suffering and the contexts in which they have experienced their suffering, most often considered a result of such issues as poverty, racism, and war. The purpose and focus of liberation psychology is to encourage active participation in social, economic, and ecological change. This can be done by nurturing an imagination of alternative ways of thinking and acting together to change the old ideas about previously invisible populations, like children. At its core, it seeks to rehumanize our beliefs and institutions that have been made invisible after generations of normalization.

When held within a patriarchal, colonizing mindset, the teacher-student relationship at any age level is one where the end result is oppression and alienation of the student rather than of freedom and inquiry. Freire named this approach the "banking concept of education," [82] where students are assumed to be ignorant, empty vessels, and teachers are assumed to be knowledge holders who bestow information to students. The action available to students in this scenario is to receive deposits of information, memorize them, and repeat them back to the teacher. The student becomes the ignorant object and the teacher the all-knowing subject. This singular aspect has the most far-reaching impact on the individual's creativity, autonomy, and self-love.

ROLE OF DEPTH PSYCHOLOGY IN EDUCATION

Depth psychology seeks to examine the underlying motives of behavior, as it has to do with the unconscious mind, our deep psyche. It is also related to the activation of human imagination; it explores and encourages imagination. The perspective of depth psychology deconstructs the colonial paradigm through specific concepts such as individuation, the transcendent function, seeing-through, and cultural restoration. The transcendent function is a means through which the arts can be used to bridge a given duality, thereby allowing a greater perspective and a "disidentification"[83] with the prevailing construct. Further, there is the archetypal act of seeing-through as a way of

---

[82] Freire, 1970/2005, p. 72
[83] Schulman-Lorenz & Watkins, 2005, p. 19

recognizing common language and rhetoric that supports oppression. Seeing-through can be used as a path toward cultural restoration, a way to imagine cultural practices that can gain freedom from the dominant, oppressive influence. [84]

There are concepts from psychology that pertain to the classroom experience, such as the healthy and pathological intellect, the transitional object, good-enough mothering, and mirroring. Jungian concepts of the psyche, such as persona, shadow, transference, archetypes, and the collective unconscious may be valuable in creating a depth pedagogy that would foster deep teacher reflectivity and existentially sensitive teaching practices. Elevating the search for meaning and transformation are reasonable goals for children in school, and may be improved by their application. Teachers trained in such psycho-spiritual pedagogy would be creators of vibrant, personal and soul-feeding classroom experiences that can lead to a more positive life view and goal setting beyond merely graduating, but creating a good life. This takes public school into the realm of resistance to the corporate threat to teachers and students' humanity. Through relationship in this environment, individuality of thought and action is fostered as a response to normalized marginalization.

In calling for the invitation of Eros into the classroom, Freud was inviting in not erotic libido, but rather "Eros as pleasure having been transformed into the psycho-spiritual passion for deeper communication with others, the universe, and the divine."[85] It is a higher principle

---

[84] Pulice, 2010
[85] Mayes, 2007, p. 127

of relatedness. Teachers' self-esteem can suffer from ideological oppression as well. Many teachers I interviewed chose the classroom over more lucrative or distinguished careers because of the call to the spirit and a desire to lift up the lives of young people. Infusing higher ideals elevates the teacher as well as the student.

INDIGENOUS/NATURAL CHILD

To educate a human being in accordance with her indigenous knowing is about rediscovering, or discovering for the first time since very early childhood, a way of being that is suppressed in conventional education: ignoring physical discomfort to sit all day, and not acknowledging or actively suppressing the feeling self. Denying one's impulses against what is being taught or how it is taught amounts to an early burying of the intuitive, embodied, feeling self. Modern education does not prepare us to sit with the mystery and complexity of direct experience. Rather, it distills that experience into disconnected ideas that live in the head and not in the heart. Life by its very nature is full of seeming contradictions, which calls for depth psychology, imagination, and a loving acceptance of a complex worldview that may include his/her own indigenous knowing.

There is a bias toward science and empiricism, where mystery may be seen as a sign of intellectual weakness, where holding paradox is viewed as an inconvenience, or foolishness. Any circumstance involving perplexity seems to demand an immediate solution; no one teaches us how to sit with an enigma in wonder. And rather than giving children the tools to connect with a complex reality, standardized answers actually make us less available to it. How did we get here? Via an educational system that fails to acknowledge the intimate mystery of nature, both outside of and within the self, and that fails to teach children to pause to feel between the question and the answer.

Children clearly feel called to their uniqueness from an early age, but many are systematically taught to ignore and suppress it. As they learn to deafen themselves to the deep messages that come to them from the world, they have to create an internal guide—an internalized oppressor that enables the colonized to colonize him/her. Detachment from the present, bowing to authority, and inability to be vulnerable are the results.

Psychological health necessitates nurturing the imagination both as a biological need and as a form of effectively nurturing the genius of childhood as a common human possession. Children are engaged in a silent dialogue between themselves and the world, as they are constantly questioning the world they live in. If we adults can become good stewards in supporting the child's sense of wonder by encouraging and hosting their questions, we will come to know that both child and adult are like-minded. The child's natural proclivity to wonder, question, and therefore imagine is seen as his or her genius. Biologically, if fostered, wonder affects the central nervous system's responses to the external world that is then responsible, adaptable, and flexible for creativity and thinking, and therefore learning. Perception is regarded for its relationship to intuition, considered as "a type of 'seeing,' stimulating in turn the organizing process we call imagination."[86] Compassion is the natural result of a supported sense of wonderment and imagination. An ever-increasing cultural complexity relies more and more on the relationship of language to metaphor, and the intuitive leaps that are the realm of genius.

At heart, metaphoric thinking is about seeing the likeness between one thing and another, or in the case of a child, between self and other. Play is, at heart, a dialogue with metaphor. Extended to the child and his or her relationship with the world, be it great or small, play and wonderment allow for the ability to feel into what is other than one's self (as opposed to Others), which is the root of love and compassion. This deeply influenced my studies because it grounded the very philosophy out of which my research sprang: the admittance of love into the relationships between student and parent, student and teacher, parent and teacher, and so on, and the experience had by all those witness to the educational system and/or environment.

Modern educational practices may be missing the mark because of the perception of children's natural inclination to play and their relationship with the imagination. Viewing play, imagination, and magical thinking as non-productive, with the idea that this is merely a phase in childhood that will soon dwindle, is in itself an error in thinking.

It is not nature that mistakenly created us to learn through play but, rather, it is our cultural and collective response to it that misses the boat. With the advent of

---

[86] Cobb, 1977, p. 47

agriculture, industry, and technology, play is no longer an effective use of time and resources. It is important to understand there are long-term effects and far-reaching qualities of the imagination and creativity when supported.[87] What we choose to empower in children as opposed to what we overpower in them works to shape the oppressive and productive nature of our Western human tradition. Indeed, we are all empowered and we are all disempowered, in that we possess abilities and we are all limited in the attempt to use our abilities. [88]

DEPTH PSYCHOLOGY AND ALTERNATIVE EDUCATION

Depth psychology utilizes the art of inquiry as seeking understanding and making meaning—both as a way of seeing and of being seen. It assumes an active, reciprocal relationship with the world, one that seeks knowledge and is receptive to knowledge that seeks us.[89] The current practices in our educational system fail to see through to the soul of the child, and to the inborn spark of genius that may enrich our world in new ways. Such a depth view provides a way in which to transform a surface-level approach to learning into an integrated relationship between world-as-teacher and student-as-world.[90]

Love and fear can be seen as the greatest drivers of all human behavior and learning. Orienting our society around our most loving nature rather than our fear is the most sane response to the question of best practices

---

[87] Pulice, 2010
[88] Kincheloe & McLaren, 2003, p. 411
[89] Coppin & Nelson, 2005, p. 11
[90] Pulice, 2010

for human development. And it enhances our chances of survival in a future whose uncertainty requires empathy and cooperation. Fear increases our separation and alienation, and begets inhumanity and violence toward those perceived to be our enemies, a population that only grows larger with such a mindset. Educating children toward their own loving, empathic capacity is rewarding and enjoyable both in the moment as well as creating a world we can all look forward to. Love wants what's best for the loved one at each moment...A *decision* and a commitment that you make every day...A *skill* that is cultivated. [91]

An excellent practice of depth psychology is inner child work, which can be an opportunity to heal our own early oppressive wounds. It is known that trauma and oppression split us off from love by separating us from our own inner child, and the cure for this split, the way to healing and integration, is through love. Adults must connect with their own history of suffering in schools, and bring such consciousness to education, in order to stop perpetuating an oppression many simply accept. First healing ourselves as adults allows us to change systems now that may still be creating such damage.

---

[91] Schiraldi, 2001, p. 72

What Student Experience Tells Us

MY RESEARCH GOAL WAS to determine whether children in modern public schools are largely a colonized people moving within a colonial system, and what damage this might be doing. Working from a depth psychological perspective, with the frame of liberation psychology, several key terms—oppression, colonization, hegemony— appeared to accurately describe the treatment of and regard for children in much of the modernized world.

My quandary was that, if in fact our children are colonized, my participants would have been made to believe the public school process was God-ordained, not to be questioned, even in their best interest. I wondered where I might find young people who were capable of reflexivity, able to critically looking at their own experience of schooling. Having sent my own children to the Middle School, which instills self-reflection, original thinking, and the knowledge that all aspects of the self have value, this seemed like the obvious choice to find participants. My additional requirement was that each had gone on to attend a public high school. As it turned out all ten participants who volunteered were white women eighteen to twenty years old who had attended Santa Barbara Middle School. As it is a private school of approximately 140 students in grades six through nine, most came from middle to upper-middle class families. All but one of the students attended the public secondary school in a downtown setting, where the population of roughly 2,200 students is approximately 40 percent white and 60 percent Hispanic, and of mixed socioeconomic classes drawn from the immediate area.

I contacted twenty individuals, seven male and thirteen female, via Facebook. I told them about my research topic, and immediately received ten replies from all female respondents. Quantitative data were collected via a survey that compared their experiences at both schools. Qualitative data were gathered through expanded, in-depth interviews and provided further exploration and explanation. By looking at both qualitative and quantitative data, I was able to gain a more comprehensive understanding of the material than if I were to employ either a survey or an interview alone. The combination of two contrasting forms of data collection neutralizes the weakness of bias that is sometimes associated with a singular source of data collection.[92]

During the interview, I asked participants to elaborate on experiences that varied between the schools so I could better understand their differences. If time allowed, I moved to questions where they had reported no difference, as a way to structure the in-person interviews. Each

---

[92] Creswell, 2014

interview was roughly one hour long. Once the interview was complete, I transcribed the recording, and a copy of their transcript was sent to the participants for their verification of its accuracy, and to increase their sense of inclusion in the process. Once they responded, I began to analyze the interview material.

METHODOLOGY

The method I used to guide my inquiry combined hermeneutics and heuristics. I approached each situation with a beginner's mind, free of any expectation or desiring of specific outcomes. When one queries with a beginner's mind, it disarms Western scientific material prejudice, which is distinctly adult-oriented and situated against the child. There is a tacit knowing that is engaged—a way of knowing closer to the ways and means of a child's learning process through imagination, intuition, instinct, fantasy, and play. To know the child's experience, one must remember the essential child's psyche existing within. Ironically, I once made the off-hand comment that this project needed to be researched and written from the eight-year-old in me. Clearly, I was on to something.

The child's imagination requires engagement. In its natural state, it cannot relate to separation, or an I-It perspective. To the Western eye, the child's psyche is all about illusion. Within the realm of play there is the tendency to interpret fantasy as illusion, and therefore out of touch with reality. However, when looked at non-literally, one sees that the child engages in fantasy and play as a way of mirroring the world around her, thus enhancing possibility for the future. Simply put, the child uses play and fantasy as ways to create connections and thereby empathic resonance with the world she helps to create.

HERMENEUTICS

The motif and method of a hermeneutics is that of the circle. In fact, the circle itself provides the child a specific way of learning and knowing as well as a way of being known. Understanding involves a continual reference to that which is already known, and operates in a circular, dialectical fashion. As we know, facts are partially constituted by their context and by their interpreter. They can only be evaluated in relation to the larger structure of theory or argument of which it is a part, at the same time, this larger structure is dependent on its individual parts.[93] Further, the circle represents the child's tendency for evolution and innovation rather than the repetition of a previously taken pathway.

Hermeneutics felt like the best approach when inquiring about a topic as personal, multifaceted, and often invisible as the experience of oppression in school. This method was particularly relevant to my inquiry into the educational system's either oppressive or positive development of the highly personal and subjective characteristics of self-knowledge, love, and connection as perceived by young people. Hermeneutics enabled a widening of the lens while at the same time valuing as essential the researcher's participation in and involvement with the topic. Hermeneutics opened up the diversity of

---

[93] Woolfolk, Sass, & Messer, 1988, p. 9

voices and amplified them. This approach echoed the need of children for more agency, subjectivity, and freedom to consider the broader context of their experiences, and to communicate their multiple perspectives.

To accomplish this, I read the interviews and engaged a circular process that involved understanding both the general themes and their meaningful parts. This circular process was most fitting when trying to understand the complexity of human motivation and social behavior, which is often rendered to the unconscious shadows. The idea that there are universal truths about any one subject is a culturally derived assumption. Quantum physics has proven that the researcher herself affects the outcome of any research; thus, the idea of validity itself is relative to the context of the researcher's own orientation.[94] What the hermeneutic method loses in the traditional idea of validity norms, it gains in terms of an invitation for multiplicities, dimensionalities, and marginalized points of view.

HEURISTICS

Heuristic research is an intimate process of meaning-making through the researcher's direct engagement with the material at hand.[95] The researcher becomes a subject of inquiry rather than a blank slate perusing objective materials. My own experience as a young female student who felt oppressed in the school classroom gave me a fertile passion for and a path of entry into my subject matter. My years of counseling and parenting included many stories of

---

[94] Goswami, 2000
[95] Douglass & Moustakas, 1985

young children who have suffered in education; this served to sensitize my ears and eyes to the world of my chosen topic. Heuristics encouraged me to stay tender and open-hearted in my own personal discovery, which lent an honest compassion to the discovery of the others I worked with in intimate research. Through rigorous self-inquiry, I found the numinous layers of psyche within myself. Through my own journey to self-understanding, the research opened portals to the communal psyche and to the shared world of the self.

In looking at the indigenous or natural child and how best to grow young humans, I began with my own educational experience. Heuristics was the research frame that supported my reflections. Then I utilized hermeneutics to guide me in the process of relating what I found on reflection, with the experience of my participants, as I moved through the research process. In other framing, heuristics invited me to include my experience as I walked the hermeneutic circle of the larger project, which served to situate my experience in context.

In my first reading of each of the transcripts I underlined sections that seemed to pop from the page, where the participants spoke of feelings, values, stories, and specific experiences that either motivated or distressed them. This provided a preliminary discovery of data as they initially began to emerge, without editing or critiquing what I found. In this way I began the hermeneutic process of allowing the themes to show themselves, rather than looking for content areas I hoped or expected to find. By the time I had read through all of the interviews in this fashion, I began to feel similar tendencies and themes being expressed by most of the participants relative to their sense of positive and negative experiences at both schools.

As I read the transcripts for the second time, I recorded essential ideas being expressed from important quotes into rough groupings, with an open possibility of what may emerge. Some groupings collected long lists, while others held only one or two quotes. I continued through the transcripts, grouping them until all had been considered, which ended up being represented by a few dozen key words and ideas presented below. (Table 1, p. 110)

I reviewed my themes, honing them into two poles of experience, Liberatory and Oppressive, with four essential Liberatory findings that fell into categories of care, connection, community, and choice. At the opposite pole of these findings were Oppressive categories of neglect, alienation, a focus on extrinsic academic value, and colonization.

I coded the data and created a data summary, an interpretation outline tool that allowed me to look at the outcomes in a deeper way, where I could question each of the findings and begin to consider explanations for each result. This method utilized critical thinking and reflection on each of the issues, including problem posing, which is an inductive questioning process rooted in the works of Lindeman, Dewey, and Piaget, who were advocates of an experiential and dialogical education. Friere used problem-posing dialogue as a means to develop critical inquiry and understanding of experience.[96] This process of working with the data in a dialogical yet structured way brought a new understanding of the similarities and differences

---

[96] Bloomberg & Volpe, 2008, p. 129

among participants' data as well as the frequency with which each theme was introduced. This helped to reinforce the relevance of the findings.

INITIAL THEMES FOUND

Liberatory Themes—MS	Oppressive Themes—HS
1. Respected by teachers	1. Felt invisible (too many kids)
2. Community building	2. No sense of school or class community
3. Valued for all qualities of self	3. Valued only for academics
4. Freedom	4. Told what to learn (banking model)
5. Support from teachers and staff	5. Overwhelmed (teachers don't care)
6. Taught values, learned about self	6. Social rank
7. Choice in what to learn (electives)	7. Need to conform
8. Deep connections	8. Expectation not known
9. More learning styles	9. No connection or relationships with teachers
10. Friends with teachers (first names)	10. Learning disability
11. Teachers learn from kids	11. Assembly line
12. Good teachers	12. Feeling worthless and depressed
13. Develop self-confidence	13. "You just had to do it that way"

Table 1

110

Some Caveats

Education is crucial for the evolution of all societies. We educate children so they can become productive, cooperative members of the adult world, contribute to their community, parent their own children, and become self-realized, happy members of the larger social body. Although our educational system may seem to have been designed toward these ends, serious questions have emerged relative to its efficacy and its impact on students as they move through it. Recent efforts to fix academics in the United States have focused on testing, forcing more curriculum onto teachers' over-full plates, and jettisoning non-academic subjects (e.g., the arts, character and social-emotional learning) because it is unclear how they impact the economic bottom-line of a capitalist culture. Non-academic learning does not seem important for creating the kind of citizens most likely to keep the nation competitive on the world economic stage.

John Lennon once said, "Our society is run by insane people for insane objectives. I think we're being run by maniacs for maniacal ends and I think I'm liable to be put away as insane for expressing that. That's what's insane about it." [97] The more I explore how children are treated in our adult-run systems, the more I have come to believe that young people who feel out of alignment in the current system of education, and within the current paradigm of adult-child relationship, are indeed those canaries in the coal mine.

Einstein famously stated that problems cannot be solved from within the same paradigm in which they were created, and this is the approach of liberation psychology: to question not just the actions being taken to accomplish a certain end, but to question the thinking that led us to choose those actions. My aim has been to look at American education through a frame of liberation psychology in order to determine two things: whether public school is a colonizing influence on children, and where oppressive processes are found, whether they create psychological and emotional harm, or undermine some of the positive goals of that educational system. I examined this question by comparing and contrasting the experiences of students who attended a private middle school that intentionally created an environment of freedom and choice, love, community, and healthy attachment—all factors that directly oppose forces of oppression—and then moved into a standard public high school environment. The middle school's humanistic education model represents liberatory educational practices, while the high school's standard public education model represents an oppressive one.

[97] BBC interview between P. Lewis and J. Lennon, 1968

My results demonstrate that the former model enfolds into its approach a humanizing love for each child, an appreciation of soul, the indigenous child, and inclusive Othering, while the latter has a competitive, oppressive, colonizing effect that gives rise to exclusionary Othering. The qualities of each approach impact the relationships between students and educators and between students and other students. Ultimately, this is what made the most dramatic difference in participants' experiences of these two schools.

While it is unthinkable at some level that we may oppress our young, when the problem is viewed through this critical lens, an oppressive dynamic emerges, and it becomes clear we need to question traditional assumptions about what education really is. As much as this reality is heartbreaking, it allows for better explanations for the epidemic increases in ADHD, anxiety, depression, drug abuse, suicide, and violence we have seen in our youth at the exact same time that our educational system has become less ensouled and more narrowly focused on the ability to process information quickly and cognitively. Such emphasis often boils down to one small aspect of cognitive processing—namely, the ability to take in and regurgitate information in order to perform well on tests. A system built around this emphasis leaves no room for lasting, deep learning that serves the child beyond the next round of tests or the end of the next grading period.

NATURE OF THE STUDY

In pursuing an understanding of whether students experienced the educational system at the public high school as oppressive, I realized that many students may have no point of comparison. Those without an experience of any other educational practices would consider it all perfectly normal. That is one of the symptoms of true colonization: the oppression appears to be either an effort to help the colonized, or it is made to seem as though it is God's will and the natural order of things. Asking someone who has been brought up in a particular system how that system has affected them is like asking a fish to describe what it is like to be in water.

Further, I suspected that even if students I interviewed did notice oppressive practices, they would not be able to question those practices nor articulate the experience fully, having been asked to conform to standards imposed upon them their entire school careers. This led me to select participants for this study who had attended the middle school for all or part of grades six through nine before moving on to the high school. Because two of my three children had attended both schools, I knew students at the middle school had been encouraged to self-reflect and express their perspectives and ideas, and that they were comfortable sharing with adults.

I discovered that my graduate program has roots in the Confluent Education program at University of California, Santa Barbara, the program that gave rise in part to the methods employed at the middle school. Using a dialogical interpretation of texts that consider the experience of oppression and colonization, as well as a hermeneutic research method, I was able to bring together my personal experience and the experience of my participants with diverse educational approaches in a way that illuminated an oppressive influence of modern public education.

Through conversation on specific themes, I was able to learn the perspective of students themselves regarding both humanistic and traditional public school methods. I have been able to gain access to their experience through the use of descriptive, feeling-toned language, and thereby sought to understand the meanings of the main threads that emerged.

This method is built on the same foundations as the liberatory teaching processes described in this study—processes that include connection and relationship with students, where shared meaning is co-created in unity of content and method and where the situation is expressed from the viewpoint of the participant. I found a degree of self-awareness was created through this process. Participants had the opportunity to reflect on events and experiences that they drew value from and may not have been aware of previously. I shared the final product of the research with students, and many reported having had light bulbs go on, increasing their understanding from a more mature perspective on the life lessons gained from the least expected elements of their experience.

Additional Considerations

One potential limitation to the study is the fact that all members of the population I studied attended the middle school, which could indicate a more progressive parenting practice at home. This could have introduced a bias toward a more liberatory perspective on schooling. In seeking to find a population where a comparison was possible with the experience of public school, I may have interviewed a unique population who were not only preferring humanistic education but who possessed more of an awareness of such differences. Another limiting factor in this study was the fact that despite my having attempted to recruit both male and female participants, all students who ultimately ended up participating were female. The female experience may not match the male experience in these two institutions.

In addition, I discovered an unanticipated variable in the research that warrants discussion. Most of the students who went from the middle school to the public high school enrolled in one of two arts academies that created an environment that mitigated some of the factors that were experienced as oppressive. Having seven of ten participants enrolled in academies (one for visual art and design, and one for multimedia art and design) may have limited the study by reducing the impact of the transition between the middle and high school environments. However, the results still speak to a dramatic difference between these students' experiences at both schools, even for those in the academies.

Three participants responded on the written survey that they experienced little or no difference between the two schools. Yet, during the in-depth interview, they described significant differences. Giving a casual interview immediately afterward to inquire more fully into their experience revealed this expectancy-effect artifact, and minimized the limitations this survey might place on the significance or generalizability of the findings, especially because I did not use the numerical findings as data.

What is Needed

When I began transcribing the interviews, I noticed frequent use of "like," "you know," and "um" peppered throughout the young women's and to a lesser extent my own speech. After spotting sixteen uses of the word "like" in the first paragraph I transcribed, I felt this was significant. Merriam-Webster's *Dictionary* defines the word "like" as follows: "used interjectionally in informal speech often to emphasize a word or phrase (as in "He was, like, gorgeous") or for an apologetic, vague, or unassertive effect (as in "I need to, like, borrow some money"; Merriam-Webster's online dictionary, n.d). Frequent use of the word "like" in this way suggests a lack of personal authority around what one knows. This language pattern created a sense of participants saying something they absolutely know for certain, and then undercutting it with their language. In many cases, they contradicted themselves without seeming to notice. This spoke of a potential colonization, where freedom of speech is restricted.

CONNECTION

Participants reported that teachers at the middle school cared about them and respected them more than at the public school, which directly affected their respect for the teacher, their attendance, and their interest in the class.

> "Just, you're never really treating teachers like they're superior except the general respect you have to have in the classroom. ...I like it better when I have a personal connection with them." (RM).

> "Just like I said before, there weren't any personal connections I had with teachers at the High School...so they definitely didn't know my experiences. ...It was definitely really hard for me to adjust after I left Middle School to go to the High School. It was really hard for me academically, I just, I started failing all my classes right away because I wasn't used to doing homework, or, um, and then I felt really overwhelmed by the amount of people, not knowing everyone, it was definitely really hard." (RM)

They also reported that the middle school's approach made it possible for intimate peer-to-peer connections where students felt unafraid of judgment or bullying and were comfortable being fully themselves at school. This sense of belonging enabled them to better apply their energies to learning and personal growth.

At the high school, students often felt lost in a sea of strangers. Social connections were difficult to forge, and most participants reported an underlying climate of divisiveness and a fear of being both disregarded and judged. Most teachers seemed overwhelmed with their workload and the number of students for whom they were responsible, and did not have the wherewithal to make direct personal connections with students. These participants, having experienced those connections— both teacher-to-student and peer-to-peer—as enormously productive in middle school, strongly felt this difference.

At the middle school, participants felt their teachers were also friends. They felt a loyalty and an attachment that inspired them to apply themselves to learning. School trips reinforced an already-present sense of trust and mutual regard between peers and teachers. This environment created willingness to participate in class discussions and to otherwise be an active participant in the learning process. Students perceived that teachers cared about them and knew personal details about their lives that were then integrated into the way those teachers interacted with them in school—a hallmark of whole-child education and of a secure attachment between teacher and student.

As students experienced a lack of this connection at the high school, they felt disappointment, but did not blame teachers. One teacher at the high school was the exception that proved the rule: He found a way to deeply connect with students, and his classroom was one where abundant learning took place (and students enjoyed themselves in the process). The character of the interaction between adult and child is extraordinarily important, and teaches the practice of attending to and responding to the other.

This is the essential feature of caretaking, and the basis of all continuing psychological growth. All growth occurs within emotional connections, not separate from them.[98]

What makes an oppressive form of education possible is an environment mostly devoid of caring relationship between educators and students. When teachers cannot authentically connect with students, an environment is created where students find it harder to connect authentically with each other. These young people feel unhappy, unsafe, and lack confidence about who they are inside and out, and so learning is hampered. As one of my research participants, Sara, explained, "Feelings are not welcome in the classroom. I went through a terrible breakup with a guy who was stalking me; I was a wreck. I walked into class crying and was basically told to just 'suck it up.' Schools need to take better care of their students."

By association, an oppressive educational system's impact on teacher-student relationship also impacts relationships between students. This does not occur because teachers do not care or because they do not want to authentically connect with students. They, like the students they teach, are operating within an oppressive system. Although their perspectives were not a part of this study, through subsequent research with the public high school teachers, I have come to believe they are equally oppressed and crave changes that would allow them the time to more deeply connect with students, their administrators, and with the subject matter they teach.

---

[98] Miller, 1979/1981, p. 15

COMMUNITY

Both the smaller school environment at the middle school and the smaller subgroups created at the high school through the arts academies allowed the participants to enjoy being known by a community. They expressed tremendous value in feeling a part of something that gave them identity and purpose. At the middle school, students had a strong sense of shared ethics and mutual respect between teachers and students. Knowing each other well and having a sense of wanting to do well as part of the community, students did not feel drawn to break rules or act out.

> *S*: "And I'm wondering, was there a sense at the middle school that people are going to try to abuse things, because there was a lack of the same strictness?"

> *ZF*: "Yeah, probably. If you know that you're being trusted to be a certain way, then you're more likely to be that way 'cause you feel like, "Okay, well, they trust me, so I don't need to break that trust. There's no reason to be rebellious and ditch class and stuff like that." And because everyone knows you, it would be very obvious if you were wandering around campus. Like everyone would know, like, "What are you doing?"

> "I felt like at the middle school we were, you know, relatively well-behaved, and I think that's a lot due to the community and just kind of all the teachers' involvement, and so when that involvement and kind of respect as I was saying earlier, seems to be lacking, I think that, I don't know, that causes more, you know, more

skipped classes or "Let's throw things at the teacher." (GH)

At the high school, a sense of alienation and lack of shared values led to separation. This environment produced a sense of isolation, which led some participants to give up on making connections. They felt that this was the way it had to be due to the larger student body.

"I think that the biggest fault of the high school is that everyone's separate and everyone is completely unaware." (ME)

"The middle school is awesome, like I learned all those values from the middle school and how to be in community and how to interact. But the high school was just like, "Okay, here is a large group of people," and like it taught me exactly the type of people I didn't want to be around and it taught me exactly how many people are willing to just be in the world in no specific way. Like learning that existing is gray, you know." (ME)

In this setting, students felt no one was tracking them, that no one was available for support when they struggled academically, and that cheating and rule-breaking were viable options.

AQ: "No one is tracking me except for, like, my parents."

S: "But would they know if you actually learned, versus memorized, versus cheated?

AQ: No…As long as I get good grades."

S: "Okay, one is learning, one's memorizing and then forgetting, and then one is just getting the answer from somewhere and getting it on the page."

AQ: "Yeah. Like my mom only cares about, like, good grades and stuff. It's, like, as long as I got good grades, it was fine."

Students spoke about their experience of the difference during the transition between the two schools:

> "So, like, in my biology class, it was in the morning, I don't even know if he knew my name, I mean he probably did but it doesn't stand out to me that he was, like, "hey, KA!"… if I saw him in the hallway later, you know what I mean? I know he had several classes and you just came in, and I felt like he was so flustered and was, like, okay, we're going to watch a video today, or here is what we are going to do today…it wasn't like, "do you understand?"… and that was my first class in high school and, like, I remember there was this one girl, this Hispanic girl who was just kind of rude and I was like, oh my goodness, people are talking in class and everyone is texting and I was just like, "oh, *what*?" I didn't know everyone in the class and it was a bunch of mixed grades and it was just, I don't know how to explain it. Luckily, I made friends but you were just kind of, like, you have to work harder to understand what's going on because the teacher is not going to help you." (KA)

This finding involved the difference between an intimate school community with known, shared, lived positive values, and one where alienation and separateness are more common experiences. A sense of community was lacking at the high school for all participants in this study, although the high school academies gave students participating in them some sense of the togetherness and connection that characterized the middle school experience. One academy participant, however, felt excluded from her academy community as well as from the larger school community, which actually felt worse for her than it might have been to only feel isolated within the larger population of the high school.

Participants reported having felt much more concerned about being seen as weird in their non-academy classes, which made them hesitant to speak out. The strong academic focus of the high school left little time or resources for a focus on values-setting, group bonding, and emotion—both of which, at the middle school, had a chance to emerge in the context of relationship. In this high school and in many others like it, the notion that emotional health and a sense of belonging are pivotal in the educational process hardly merits a blip on the radar. Humanistic education, however, dictates that without a feeling component, no real learning can take place since schools are social places and learning is a social process. Students do not learn alone but rather in collaboration with their teachers, in the company of their peers, and with the support of their families. Emotional well-being can either help or hinder children's learning and their ultimate success in school. Because social and emotional factors play such an important role, schools are realizing they must attend to this aspect of the educational process for the benefit of all students. [99]

In the case of the public high school, a lack of social and emotional values, or guidance and support from teachers, left students fighting for a spot in the power hierarchy, creating a pecking order, and navigating a fear-based environment. The peer oppression became as strong a factor at the high school as the system itself.

> "I felt I was judged so much more at the high school. Like, I don't know, I felt like I would just, like, walk around and stuff and just be— like no one would really see me sometimes. I felt invisible because there's so many people." (AQ)

CARE

The frequency and depth of explanation of the participants' value toward a whole-child education at the middle school was highly significant and stands out as the strongest finding in the study. From electives to their annual music festival, to the highly valued weeklong bike trips, the non-academic learning was the most powerful for participants. Even though they reported that the trips were extremely difficult and they often did not enjoy them, students' ultimate valuation of those experiences provided the most significant finding due to the number of participants who talked about them, as well as how many times the trips came up. Despite the fact that I never asked a question about the trips, they invariably were spoken of with great

---

[99] Zinns, Bloodworth, Weissberg, & Walberg, 2004, p. 3

emotion and energy, and they generated the greatest sense of self-esteem and self-awareness of all aspects of both schools combined.

"So, I learned positive reinforcement for myself and for others. On the trips I was cold a lot, I was tired a lot, but I enjoyed myself and I enjoyed connecting with other people and I enjoyed, like, to be myself and be really dirty and really ugly and it was kind of funny, and then I like to sing and I like to make weird dances with my friends and, I don't know, it's like super, like you figured out what you were like." (RP)

"You go on these trips with teachers and you call them by their first name. And, yeah, you just know all about them, their lives. A lot of them are middle school alums. So they've just been there their whole life, and yeah. You don't know much personally about teachers at the high school. Like I didn't know anything personal about any of my teachers there…it's generally, like, harder to get to know them if there's just this wall up that they're superior. …And then in middle school you're sort of, like, doing the same things, you're on the trips together, sort of, like, in families for the dinners." (RM)

"Like, I feel like people would even do stuff with their teacher outside of school and they would have, you know…middle school would have bike rides or swims or something, you would see your teachers a lot more." (MD)

"Yeah, and we would go on those trips together and the weekly meetings, and I feel like the school's energy was just a lot more caring and personal." (MD)

Participants reported an overwhelming emphasis on grades and test scores at the high school. Prioritizing product (grades, test scores) over the process of learning led participants to feel less enthusiastic about learning. Some became cynical about the overall purpose of school.

S: "You're saying the system allows for cheating, in a sense?"

AQ: "Yeah. It's so easy. Like, I wouldn't cheat as much as everyone else did. Like people would cheat, like, every test. Yeah, a lot...."

S: "Is cheating common at the middle school—do you recall that?"

AQ: "I don't, I don't really remember, like, cheating at all."

S: "Right, okay. So does it feel that when the right answer is the goal, it encourages cheating? Like, not about your process, and that was more the goal?"

AQ: "Yeah, because it's just, like, 'Get the right answer on the page and, like, get the good grade and, like, that's what matters.' Just like super-mechanical."

"English class freshman year, she thought we were all idiots and wanted us to shut up and, like, we had to fill out a sheet and I cheated on it for sure. It was *asking* me to cheat. Aubrey and I. Across the classroom...me and Deb had a signal. Like A was that (knocking), B was that, C was that, you know?" (RP)

"Well, I mean in high school you're a class, you're a student among other students and of course you're with your friends and stuff, but you know, they don't appreciate you as an individual as much as you as a student doing a good job, you know. They don't value you for anything else other than that, really. I mean, unless, you know, the teacher is more open. In most cases I'd say it's not that way. It's not like that, you know." (WP)

When school is all about getting a good grade, and when that good grade is given not in response to one's engagement with ideas or creativity but in response to simply regurgitating the right answers on a test, what is taking place may not even be definable as learning. To these students whose previous school experience focused on process over product, this felt uncomfortable, even insulting, but also like a necessary requirement for admission into college.

S: "If we're not looking to blame anyone for why it's that way…does that make you feel that the way public school is set up is just to ask you to spit out the right answer and they don't care if you learn?"

WP: "How does that make me feel?…I think it's disappointing that they would set up a system like that where how you 'learn' is by just giving the right answer. I don't know, it's stupid."

S: "Do you feel like you only learn when you do things right, or do you sometimes learn when you do things wrong?"

WP: "Well, that's bullshit, you can't only learn things doing them right. That's not true."

S: "So it feels like grades are what matters at the public high?"

WP: "Absolutely. There is nothing else that matters. In the big picture, obviously you are worried about your ego and your friends and stuff like that, but school, high school, it's all about the grades. There is nothing else. At least there is nothing else on *my* mind. You can't even think about college if you can't get good grades."

S: "And college is the only goal?"

WP: "Well, they, they have taught you to think that college is what happens when you do everything right and you get all the right answers, basically. You get all As, you go to the best college. Well then, it's, like, get As, you know? It's that kind of mentality."

These students proved that kids do in fact know the difference, they do understand, and they are hurt and insulted by a system that values their subjective wisdom with little or no regard.

ME: "And then, like, I feel you get to the high school and it was just so, like, 'Here's our lesson plan, like these are the questions of our previous years, like, this is where students get the highest scores, you know, like, so, like, answer these questions, go by this, like da-da-da-da.' You know, like, it was, like, it was just, like, 'We've done all these and we have been successful in getting our students the grades that we want so, like, do these,' you know? And it was kind of, like 'Some of these students who have followed the plan that's already worked previously.' It's, like, Okay.... Nobody did the work, no one. And so the teachers would, like, give assignments that were, like, easy enough that it was, like, those people could at least try and do something, like, get half credit or something, you know? But hard enough but they weren't even hard. It was, like, something for the ones that are actually doing it to get credit."

S: "Just do it and you'll get a good grade?"

ME: "Yeah, yeah, exactly. It's pretty depressing. You definitely feel more, like, a number. It's just kind of, like, 'Oh, here, you're in an institution, and we're just, like, going to get you through your requirements and c'mon, don't cause trouble, you know, and just do the work, we'll give you the grade, like GPA, go to college, you know, okay.'" (chuckles)

S: "What do you think the goal of the high school is—education, the schooling, the classes, what's the goal?"

AQ: "To get you out, to graduate."

S: "At the public high, it's more about right answers? And that's about you graduating?

AQ: Like, as long as you graduate, they don't really care. Like they don't even pay much attention to you until, like, three months before you graduate even. And then they're, like, 'You need this and this and this, otherwise you're not going to graduate.' It's all about that."

S: "Requirements?"

AQ: "Yeah."

S: "Okay, but I'm wondering if I'm from another planet, and what is it that they're asking you to do to graduate? You're a student, you enter, what do they think needs to happen between you and the school in order to get to the finish line? What is that in terms of what the school is doing? ...If you were to tell an alien, 'What do you have to do to get to the finish line?'"

AQ: "You just need to pass your classes—like, if you got Cs, like, they wouldn't care, you just need to pass them."

S: "How do you pass them, what's the process of passing a class?"

AQ: "You get good grades."

S: "How do you do it?"

AQ: "Study, I guess. But I never, I like, barely ever studied in high school. I just would, like, learn in class and then go take the test. I didn't even try that hard, I don't think. I could definitely have tried harder." (laughs)

S: "Right. So, getting a grade by taking a test . . ."

AQ: "Yeah, it's all about tests. It's more a [culture] of tests than anything else. In middle school we would do arts and crafts and, like, make things that had to do with our subject."

AQ: "And that's it. Their purpose there is to get you to college but it's kind of, like, the fast way. Like, not even the fast way but just, like, the straight way. You just got to get the grades, like, graduate and go to college. Not even, not even go to college, just, like, 'Make sure you graduate.'"

S: "Do you think the high school could incorporate a value that included loving and nurturing and kindness in that process?"

AQ: "Maybe. But I just feel like there's too many students."

S: "You can't have love and kindness?"

AQ: "No, 'cause the reason why there's so much of that at the middle school is because the teachers actually get one-on-one with the kids and, like, get to develop, like, a really good relationship with them."

MD: "Yeah, I feel like at the high school you were just there to get through it and it was, like, get the work done, busy work. And at the middle school it was more, a lot more, hands-on. Less testing and...less answers, really. Yeah, not as much as the high school."

S: "Well, so you're saying the middle school was more interested in you learning through a process, regardless of what you end up with?"

MD: "Yeah."

S: "And then the high school was more interested in, get to the right answer and we don't care what happens in between."

MD: "Yeah, basically. It felt like a lot of the, like, the creativity question, really, the high school didn't really encourage you to be that creative, they just wanted you to get to that answer to make it easier for themselves, really."

This finding revolves around a subjective worthiness and intrinsic value of the whole child. It's an expansion of the first two findings, integrating relationship into a larger picture where what the individual child brings to the classroom and to his or her relationships becomes an important aspect of the educational process and the culture of the school. Each student's identity, interests, strengths, and passions are made part of the life of the community. At the middle school, educational strategies, including social-emotional learning, the arts, and attention to process over product, developed non-cognitive aspects of the child that need development as much as (or more than) the relatively small part of the self that processes cognitively.

A whole-child approach inculcates knowledge of self in the child—the self that is his or hers alone, as well as the self that interacts with others. It instills a true sense of value of diverse aspects and qualities of one's self, rather than designating one's own value based on grades, getting high test scores, or getting into a good college. It guides students to see mistakes and failures as opportunities to learn within a safe container of trusted peers and teachers. Feeling a sense of belonging in school by the teacher can influence a child's self-acceptance well into adulthood. Finally, the whole-child approach integrates nature: experiences in nature, such as the bike trips and camping trips taken by students at the middle school, and a process of looking to natural systems as guides for learning. This educational approach was experienced by students as producing true learning that helped them in life.

CHOICE

At the middle school, choice was experienced as energizing and fun, and created motivation to attend class and bear with other tasks that may have been boring or mandatory. Within the humanistic model, students were able to move their bodies and use the bathroom as needed, and otherwise tend to their own physical well-being without a sense of being disruptive to the whole.

> *AQ:* "And it's fun for kids, like, it makes them, like, want to do it. Like, all kids want to—like, even when you're in junior high, all you want to do is, like, play and, like, go and screw around and stuff and, like, so doing something that wasn't, like, writing or taking notes, I don't know, like, something, like, classroom. We got to, like, go outside and, like, use our, like, heads more, and bodies. Like, we got to, like, sing and, like, act and, like, make things. Express creativity, not just thinking, 'word on page.' I think it, like, we still had to do the 'word on page' thing."

> *S:* "You combined?"

> *AQ:* "Yeah. And I think it makes you learn better. It's two different methods and that's why middle school is so great for, like, different kinds of kids because you get both sides of the way people learn. And then in middle school it was, like, 'Okay, we need to learn this, like, this is where we're going, like, it's part of a little journey.'"

> *S:* "And middle school…"

AQ: "It's more creative."

S: "How would you get that A in Marlene's class? What would you have to do?"

AQ: "I would still take a test. But the way we learned information was different. It's more, like, playing toward, like, the creative side of children and I always think that that needs to be, like, worked a little bit. It's, like, a muscle that you need to—I think that creativity is the most important thing."

Students at the high school were treated as people in need of civilizing and as empty vessels into which information must be poured in order to make them viable citizens. Most striking in this finding was the students' own lack of awareness of the contradiction in feeling a sense of gratitude for a system that they expressed as depressing, miserable, and boring, and that they did not learn from. All expressed that the academics were strong at the high school, yet they did not remember the material they memorized. This dichotomy demonstrates a colonized mindset.

S: "So tell me about how the right answer was important in high school classes. Tell me about that process and maybe even how that felt.

AQ: "I definitely felt like it was more important to get a good grade than even to learn anything. Like, this is, like, a bad thing to say, but, like, I had to, like, cheat so many times just to get, like, a good grade, just because I didn't think it was very important to learn anything. And, like, at middle school, I never did that. Like, I always found a way to, like, learn everything I was, like, learning. Like, I still remember, like, learning about, like, the Greek gods and stuff in, like, Domi's class."

"I feel, like, they orient you in the way where they are, 'Here are your requirements, we're just going to tell you a lot, what your requirements are, and then we're going to show you these classes and just really make it really clear that these classes are fitting these requirements.' You know, it's kind of, like, you're being asked to learn the materials that are certified to give you the requirements that you need to go to college—like, the A through G list, right away. And honestly, when I think back to it, I don't know how much I learned in high school except for probably two classes." (ME)

Finally, this finding was an illustration of the difference between an interactive, curiosity-based, critical thinking approach and Freire's banking model of education. While the high school's ingest-and-regurgitate model was seen by all participants as far less valuable than the humanistic approach of the middle school, It was also seen as a necessary evil. They believed somehow it would better prepare them for the real world. In the high school, students were indoctrinated into the idea that getting the right answer and performing well on tests that required little more than memorization were the most important goals. Students capable of mastering this system did well enough to move on to good colleges, but they saw it as soul-draining and of little value. They knew they were not truly learning or building character, but were completing mindless tasks to get the grade to move along in the system.

This paradox emerged in the interviews of virtually every participant in this study.

All participants saw that the more ensouled, indigenous, communitarian, whole-child, choice-full, process-oriented education they received in middle school taught them about how to be socially conscious, competent, self-connected adults. However, they also almost universally stated that the high school's approach and culture were better reflections of the real world, and they expressed gratitude they had been exposed to it. Otherwise, they implied, how would they manage that real world when they stepped into it after finishing school?

Incorporating the Four Cs in Schools

I FOUND SIGNIFICANT PATTERNS among the findings where participants, each in their own unique ways, expressed how care, connection and relationship building, and community characterized their education at the middle school, thereby creating a sense of freedom and choice. They did not experience rigorous academics at the middle school; however, they felt they still remembered even the highly academic material they studied due to the creative and experiential learning methods employed. Because everything they learned was placed in a meaningful context, they reported learning lessons about life, values, and about themselves that have been durable and continued to benefit them as they went on to college.

> "The people and the depth of conversation outside of the classroom and the purpose of, whatever, was a lot deeper in middle school. ... Our connection was less situational and more meaningful, I guess. We did things together,

like the experiences we had together even during recess or during electives were—again, maybe I'm younger, but still were way more meaningful." (RP)

"I think middle school actually, like, the whole thing it's, like, all the cheesy values, you look at them, 'Oh, that's so cheesy,' like, they actually really do stick, it's weird. Like the 'carpe diem' thing, like, the suicide swims, just, like, pushing yourself past your limits, those things stick with you. Like, I talked to so many people and all these middle school kids are, like, 'Yeah, we love pushing ourselves, and, like, going outdoors and being adventurous and, like, running into the ocean at midnight and things like that,' and people at school are just, like, 'Oh, no.' Because it's almost, like, you need to get—it's, like, an addiction to, like, living, almost—like being alive. They teach you, like, how to live, you know and, like, how to be alive in the world and it's so cool. I feel like that is something that is so often lost by something like a public school, like, 'Here are the requirements . . .' you know? I am so thankful for middle school because they pushed you, you know?" (ME)

While the participants reported the high school provided strong academics, as they spoke in more detail, they consistently felt they did not remember what they had learned. Some felt there was an unspoken norm that cheating was tolerated by teachers, either by looking the other way when it happened among students, or through a more sanctioned study guide given just before a test with all of the answers explicitly given. Students generally found the process to be primarily memorization, testing, and forgetting.

All participants reported that the oppressive dimensions of the public school were valuable in preparing them for the real world. Unanimously, they felt the real world held similarly oppressive values, and they felt that the two experiences provided a good balance for them—even after having described the high school in terms that contradicted any positive impact of that experience. The high school's academics consisted of large amounts of facts, with the load increased exponentially with Advanced Placement courses, that were memorized and given back on tests and then promptly forgotten. Even as they saw the value of this within the school system itself, they saw its absurdity—in part, because they had had a humanistic educational experience where process, interpretation, effort, and creativity mattered. Learning had relevance at the middle school, while schoolwork at the high school was tantamount to climbing rungs of a ladder to reach the goal of college.

There is such a premium placed on remembering facts, children come to believe that's what really matters—and they may even come to develop a "quiz show" view of intelligence that confuses being smart with knowing a lot of stuff. This ultimately creates citizens who can't question, and a lack a depth perspective toward life. Because learning is reduced to right or wrong answers, students may come to think that a right or wrong answer is available for all questions and problems in life, and that someone else already knows the answer to all these questions, so personal and original interpretations are not expected. The task is to find or guess the right answer, rather than to engage in interpretive activity. [100]

---

[100] Kohn, 2000, p. 18

This opens the door to some very interesting questions. Indeed, what might the real world be like if the majority of students were exposed to humanistic educational practices all the way through their schooling? Are we *creating* a certain kind of world with many undesirable qualities—where a focus on competition, hierarchical mindset and lack of social-emotional intelligence are drilled into our children—with the very educational system we have put in place? It is clear we are consciously or unconsciously doing so every day, but with awareness and a conviction to change, this trend can be turned around without great cost or training. We need a commitment to humanizing school for children and teachers alike, and to the future our youth hope to create. And we must begin the change with ourselves and how we view our children's education.

The implications are hopeful. One would think that once a dynamic that is distressing to children and reduces expression of their full potential is revealed, it would only be a matter of time before such previously invisible forces are reversed. However, in my conversation with feminist activist Gloria Steinem about my research, she recalled her own naïvete back in the 1960s when she first joined the feminist movement and imagined "that explaining it would make the necessary change."[101] Warning me of potential burnout, she described how abolition laws took 100 years to pass, women's suffrage took an equal amount of time to gain ground, and that we have much farther to go before we reach full equality for women, people of color, and children with humanitarian values.

---

[101] Gloria Steinem (personal communication, May 2, 2012)

Methods for providing children with a liberatory education do not look, at first glance, like they will give young people the advantages they need to succeed in the world. They are methods designed to cultivate loving connection, to encourage freedom in thinking and relating, learning through taking risks and making mistakes, and to teach students how to live and learn as part of a caring community—more succinctly, methods that incorporate the needs of the soul. Practices that oppose oppression are being moved into schools as social-emotional learning programs. Such programs promote connectivity, loving relationship, and inclusive Othering in environments where such elements are lacking.

Mounting evidence suggests that transforming school climate is necessary not only to promote better social, emotional, and physical health in our children, but that it is also key for making schools more successful academically. Programs that introduce humanistic principles into standard education reliably work to improve grades and student investment in school and improve students' experience of school, even when the schools themselves do not change their oppressive practices.

Changing school climate is a necessary part of improving schools' academic performance. In a 2013 study, researchers defined school climate as comprised of: (a) order, safety, and discipline; (b) academic supports; (c) personal and social relationships; (d) school facilities; and (e) school connectedness.[102] They found that school climate has a pivotal influence on whether at-risk schools beat the odds—meaning, whether schools expected to fail based on

---

[102] Voight, Austin, & Hanson, 2013

the socioeconomic status of their students achieve better than expected academically as measured by standardized tests. The study adds to the growing body of evidence that suggests that school climate is one of the factors that differentiate schools that succeed from those that do not …furthermore, the study indicates that a school's climate may have *more* to do with its success than the resources at its disposal. This result implies that things like high expectations for students, caring relationships between teachers and students, and feeling safe at school are more associated with success than teacher or administrator experience or student support services staff ratio. [103]

This suggests that any properly supported, wisely developed investment in human capital will pay for itself many times over. It may do so in ways our current capitalistic, hierarchical, unlimited growth-oriented system has no language to define, and it does not fit into our picture of what education is supposed to do. Social scientist Joshua Aaronson's research looks at how social forces shape learning and intellectual performance, motivation, and self-image, which can undermine achievement by creating a threatening social environment. His works demonstrates how even subtly changing a testing situation can reduce students' feelings of threat and dramatically improve standardized test scores and motivation. He found that we can do a lot to boost both achievement and the enjoyment of school by understanding and attending to how children experience stress and fear. The good news is making such changes has an equivalent positive effect on the adults in schools.

---

[103] Voight, Austin, & Hanson, 2013, p. 5

Bringing soul into the conversation about teaching our young makes a focus solely on extrinsic performance values like grades, test scores, and graduation rates impossible. It requires that we take a balanced perspective between intrinsic values of self-knowledge, a sense of meaning and community, and care, along with externally validated criteria. What a more ensouled education requires is taking time out of rigorous academics to instill humanistic and loving values; to create relationships with both elders and peers; to provide opportunities for students to express themselves, in addition to learned academic content in creative methods of their own design and choosing; and to give them time in nature in order to learn in an embodied way the laws of the natural world.

The goals of depth psychology are to see through the surface level of phenomena and to identify, analyze, and interpret what may appear to be explainable through conventional cultural beliefs in order to consider unconscious or previously unnoticed dynamics. This method was originally developed and used in one-on-one psychotherapy; however, it may also be used to analyze collective social systems and institutions. It is accomplished through an open-minded approach to events, with a critical, interrogative process of questioning assumptions and more obvious conclusions. In this way, unconscious underpinnings may be viewed and brought into the light of day for consideration and fresh meaning-making, using our imaginative and intuitive capacities to find new interpretations. Through the use of depth psychological approaches, we may come closer to understanding individuals and systems being researched, and better address larger issues affecting our community and society as a whole.

I welcome and include James Hillman's view that "the job of psychology is to offer a way and find a place for soul within its own field."[104] Depth psychology in particular attempts to find connections between life and soul, maintaining that "by seeing differently we do differently."[105] Through a depth psychological approach, we engage in one of the main activities of the soul, through meaning and struggle we change events into experiences. In my research, one of the greatest differences I found in these young women's experiences was this very contrast: one education system was soul-filling while the other was soul-killing. It is clear we must bring depth psychology and consideration of each person's well-being, including of the adults, into our conversation about education if we are to save our children from a self-perpetuating system that is not fully serving them. The larger concern is that, by extension, our public education is not serving our larger communities.

A depth approach also reinforces the results of my study: that through inquiry, we engage in an active, reciprocal relationship with the world. By inquiring into the lifeworld of young students, we develop the shared goals of both seeking knowledge and being receptive to knowledge that seeks us, creating a rich and rewarding environment in which to grow. Being open to the mystery and excitement at the core of true learning is a distinctly depth posture, and one that feeds the curious minds we are all born with.

---

[104] Hillman, 1976/1992, p. 55
[105] Hillman, 1976/1992, p. 122

One of the first moves to accomplishing this will require a greater sense of free time, something we have a drastic shortage of in schools.

Concepts from child development are used to consider what children need to become healthy and happy adults. When applied to education, they can be seen as forming a continuation of the parenting process, one that the community itself engages in. Psychology maintains that love, connection and attachment, a sense of belonging, and the ability to make choices within their environment are all essential elements in the growth of the child. Studies have shown that healthy attachment missed in childhood can be recovered through effective positive therapeutic relationship.[106] As there is no other non-familial adult more significant in a child's life than his or her teacher, there is an opportunity for schools to incorporate practices that prioritize relationship and attachment during the school years. When there is time in the day for teachers to mentor students in vocational projects, providing guidance and training in nonacademic learning, students thrive. Such an apprentice model creates precious time for bonding and relationship, the keys to motivation and self-worth in children.

The prospects for better emotional functioning and sense of well-being for a large portion of our population, namely children and adults in our public schools, who would benefit psychologically from such practices make this endeavor worth considering. With more families having both parents working full-time, single parenting, or working multiple jobs to make ends meet, this is an

---

[106] Wallin, 2007

increasingly important issue in our country. With increased mobility, extended family is often unavailable to take on secondary caregiving, so this task is left to schools and daycare. Having a population of securely attached young people moving into positions of power and decision-making in our community may bring a greater sense of satisfaction and increased humanity to the whole.[107]

This study is important because it asked young people themselves how our system impacted them. Most child studies and theories are based on adult research and observation, statistical results, and performance-based analysis that do not reflect students' own subjective experience of public school or the effect of the system on their psyche, sense of well-being, safety, and love of learning. In a colonial environment, the colonized are not included in the process of their education and indoctrination into the culture of the hegemony. In this case, it is the adult world that determines what best to teach our youth based on values that have been agreed upon at the state and national levels. Children themselves have not been consulted. One of the goals of this study is to give voice to those within the system so that we may begin to better understand ways we might improve education not just for young people at school, but the teachers who teach them and for society at large.

OPPORTUNITIES FOR CHANGE

It may be slow going to transform American schools. Most research agrees that sustainable change takes three to five

---

[107] Liedloff, 1975/1977

years with a strong commitment to a shared vision. I also recognize that it is possible to immediately enact some of the key findings of my research. There are small steps we can take to begin developing community among parents, teachers, and administrators, which would help to create a movement toward liberatory education practices and begin a shift in our relationship to children in our society. Small but essential changes could be achieved in a number of ways.

It can begin with a commitment by education leaders to defend teachers' need for reliable, unscheduled time during the school day to refresh themselves, and do regular self-care. Teacher burnout, comprised of emotional exhaustion and depersonalization, is a well-known problem, with almost half of all new teachers leaving the profession within five years. Teachers with a greater sense of well-being are more likely to make genuine contact with students, something participants described as missing at the public school. By improving the experience of teachers, students will reap the benefits through a more positive classroom climate. School leadership can encourage teachers who are passionate about open-minded, creative, out-of-the-box approaches to their subjects to take risks and fail, to keep their work fresh. Without such support, teachers can still practice self-care, greater connection with students and peers, and take steps to enhance their well-being. As Gloria Steinem remarked, "Every act of rebellion is important, even if unobserved."[108] By training such rebels in the methods of humanistic and loving educational processes, we may reach a tipping point where more young people

---

[108] Gloria Steinem (personal communication, May 2, 2012)

reach adulthood with these experiences to pass on to the next generation.

A teacher training program is needed that is dedicated to liberatory school practices—programs that teach simple techniques that can be incorporated easily into public classrooms to create connectedness, passion, emotional safety, and care. Feeling loved and seen as whole increases resilience, and both teachers and students benefit from such a climate. When children observe adults practicing self-care it can be a powerful lesson, and teachers creating strong community with their co-workers sets the tone that tells students school is a fun, safe space. Teaching councils, or listening circles, as a regular part of the weekly routine helps to incorporate the whole child into the learning process.

Although many SEL programs are already working with youth in schools, I use AHA! as a model because it adheres very closely to the tenets of humanistic education as described in Confluent Education and at the middle school. AHA! recognizes the importance of working not only with students to teach social-emotional competencies, but also to work with teachers who can become driving forces behind this shift.

AHA! was founded in 1999, just after the Columbine shootings. It employs an original curriculum in a mutual format where skilled adult facilitators work with teens, generally in a ratio of 1:6, as high adult mentoring ratios show the strongest impact. Students learn social-emotional skills including empathy, communication, deep listening, acceptance of others, use of creativity to express one's self, and ways to identify and cope with emotions. Surveys of students who participated in an AHA! group either in school or as an after-school activity demonstrated that the program helped them better cope with problematic areas of their lives, helped them accept others, helped them better cope with and respond productively to challenging emotions, made them less likely to fight with others, and generally helped them get along better with others (including peers and adults). It has been a part of the high school's Freshman Seminar since 2011, and the results there have been strongly positive—but not yet adequate to effect the desired change in the school's culture.

Another exciting initiative that supports a change in the culture of separateness and violence among teens in school is Restorative Approaches, a program that came to the high school in fall 2013. Restorative Approaches is a set of practices and principles designed to increase safety and interconnectedness on school campuses while providing healing avenues for restoration. RA offers alternatives to punitive responses such as suspension when rules are broken or when one student harms another. It enacts a shift from zero-tolerance discipline policies to policies that build loving relationship and restore good faith through a process sourced from indigenous wisdom. Rather than removing a perpetrator from the community for punishment, efforts are made to address the wrongdoing, involving all who were impacted, and to re-integrate the perpetrator as a contributing member of the community, building stronger, healthier networks of relationship for all involved. The high school staff and faculty have been attending weeklong seminars in order to gain the tools of Restorative Approaches, which aim to facilitate a less disciplinary mode and stronger community orientation that uses an inclusionary, respectful approach to young people who act out, break rules, or harm others at school. At one school in Walla Walla, Washington, Restorative Approaches led to an 85 percent reduction in suspensions and a drop in expulsions and written referrals by nearly half. Research in the United States and the United Kingdom is ongoing, with promising preliminary results demonstrating sizeable shifts in school culture.

AHA! also runs a unique program called PeaceBuilders, which is designed to complement Restorative Approaches. In PeaceBuilders, teens from three high schools in Santa Barbara are trained to support efforts to create greater safety on the campus. They gather for a weekend summer workshop to learn in greater depth important parts of the AHA! method—specifically, the Connection Circle format for sharing, listening, working out problems, and creating restoration where harm has been done, a format that is also integral to Restorative Approaches. The teens learn skills relating to respect, listening, communication and repair, and meet monthly to share their experiences on campus with a trained facilitator. While they are not expected to enforce any actions at school, there has been a culture change when teens who are leaders begin to practice listening, respect, and communication among their peers. This is a grassroots effort to infuse the high school with students who are well-versed in humanistic practices, and who will hopefully help to make these practices the norm on their campuses. Those who are in support of this effort, myself included, are hopeful that this club will support the building of loving community on campus, in turn improving student well-being and the school's academic standing.

The two arts academies at the high school clearly had impact on students, providing a bridge from the smaller, more nurturing environment of the middle school to the much larger, more isolating experience at the public high school. Students felt a sense of community and an increased sense of safety, connection, and fun. This news gives impetus to the idea of creating more small group structures within the larger public school setting. One student reported:

> Community is a great word for both the arts academy and middle school. There is no community involved in the high school. It's just so scattered and all over the place. It's like when you're walking down the hall you see a million people, a lot of them that you don't actually know. So, yeah, there is a level of unknown, kind of some anxiety around it because you don't know these people who are around because you don't see them every day. So you are afraid of getting judged more at the high school because there are a lot of people you don't know. And there are a lot of the same kind of kids at the middle school, the same kind of kids are in the arts academy, but you go to the high school and it's every different kind of kid you can think of. So it's not, you're not going to get the same kind of people in a normal high school class. (WP)

The students in academies were given an arts elective every semester, with project-based learning, and group/ cooperative learning. Being known by teachers and peers made a difference to the participants interviewed, giving the academies a small-school feeling despite existing within the large public system. This school within a school consistently elicited positive sensibilities that connected the students' public high school experience to that of the middle school.

Immediate action can be taken to improve the oppressive aspects of public education by bringing such programs to schools to teach social/emotional learning and mutuality. Expansion of the use of outside programs could introduce liberatory, humanistic concepts of interconnectedness and trusting in one's own indigenous wisdom. Such programs could support development of freedom of thought and creativity (all aspects of AHA!'s social-emotional learning program) in public middle and high schools. Teaching skills, theory, and practices of social-emotional learning to students, teachers, and administrators reinforces mutuality, kindness, and community.

Importantly, adults can encourage young people to challenge and ultimately dismantle structures of power that don't serve them so they can begin to shape the world around them. We can make an effort to restore the interdependence of children in the world around them, where there is a flow of power in both directions, and not just from the top down. We can insist on the inclusive dialogue of youth, where they express their desires freely and are transformed by engaged participation. Liberation Theater master Brent Blair stated that "feeling is the first step toward fighting oppression. This is a rehearsal for life!"[109] When students take action, like the students in Florida leading a movement for stricter gun laws, they

---

[109] B. Blair, personal communication, July 6, 2007

make the move from passive object to active subject; they become able to respond and therefore able to challenge the hegemony. When we are afraid of failing or of being judged, the hegemony wins.[110]

Practicing mindfulness is one way in which to engage the child's natural way of being. It can be thought of as moment-to-moment, "non-judgmental awareness, cultivated by paying attention in a specific way, that is, in the present moment, as non-reactively, as non-judgmentally, and as open-heartedly as possible."[111] Deeply phenomenological, this practice puts one in contact with the heart of the experience without the clouding tendencies of cultural bias, judgment, assumption, and expectation. Mindfulness calls on one to know the thing in itself. The practice "depend[s] on the clarity of the mind as mirror and its refined capacity to reflect, contain, encounter, and know with great fidelity things as they actually are."[112] Kabat-Zinn reflected upon sitting meditation in the following way:

> We have to understand what it means to sit. It doesn't just mean to be seated. It means taking your seat in and in relationship with the present moment. It means taking a stand in your life. ...That is why adopting and maintaining a posture that embodies dignity ...the embodiment of dignity inwardly and outwardly immediately reflects and radiates the sovereignty of your life that you are who and what you are...beyond what anybody else thinks about you, or even what *you* think about you. It is a dignity without self-assertion—not

---

[110] Pulice, 2009

[111] Jon Kabat-Zinn, 2005, p. 108

[112] Kabat-Zinn, 2005, p. 111

driving forward *toward* anything, nor recoiling
from anything—a balancing in sheer presence,
a presencing.[113]

This is the goal of guiding a child through the
educational process: to allow that child to take a stand, to
know him or herself in the deepest way possible in order to
then know the world, and to remain steadfast in self-love
and self-knowing while at once radiating outwardly a love
and empathy for all he or she encounters.[114] To approach
the topic through this lens makes the effort to reach the
child's experience through the very words, images, and
actions of that child. A mindful attitude allows us to notice
the failure of the oppressive frame of modern Western
education, offers a means to heal and restructure it, and
lastly, suggests alternatives to the alienation of our natural
imagination, which could ultimately build bridges between
a wounded cultural practice and a more indigenous way of
perceiving, living in, and living with the world.

Bestselling author (and college dropout) Paul Tough's
How Children Succeed [115] opened with a story about a
preschool classroom that utilized an unorthodox approach
called Tools of the Mind. This approach was not focused
on developing pre-academic skills related to reading and
math, but on interventions "intended to help children
learn a different kind of skill: controlling their impulses,
staying focused on the task at hand, avoiding distractions
and mental traps, managing their emotions, organizing
their thoughts." [116]

---

[113] Kabat-Zinn, 2005, p. 254
[114] Pulice, 2010
[115] Tough, 2012
[116] Tough, 2012, p. xii

Other studies have highlighted different approaches to addressing toxic stress. One school implemented a school-based mindfulness and yoga intervention. Researchers wanted to examine positive outcomes that these can have on fourth- and fifth-grade students. They selected four public elementary schools in urban communities where the program was taught four days a week with twenty-five students per forty-five-minute session. Each session included guided-mindfulness practices, breathing techniques, and yoga-based physical activities. Their findings revealed that it was effective in reducing problematic involuntary engagement responses to social stress, which the researchers defined as rumination, intrusive thoughts, emotional arousal impulsive action, and physiological arousal.

For Ongoing Study

A few participants pointed out that personality type seemed to matter in the way the students experienced the public high school. More extroverted types seemed to have an easier time making connections that improved their experience with teachers and peers, and introverted types suffered more alienation and separation. Some students have the necessary qualities to achieve in a thinking-dominant academic environment, to keep up with constant production of homework on time, and fit in socially in either setting. Those who do not, who are more introverted, feeling-oriented, and intuitive in their understanding of tasks can fall through the cracks and fail. Students in my study who succeeded academically in both systems found the public system soul-killing despite their success—they did not take it seriously, cheated to get good grades, and reported learning little of value in high school. They simply knew how to work the system and were extroverted enough to make social connections in an unwelcoming environment. Students who made the effort to create relationships with teachers seemed to fare better than those who were shy and did not make those connections. Notably, two of the high-achieving students fell ill for extended periods of time with stress-related illnesses. Self-harm, addiction, and risk-taking are less obvious but significant tolls that high achievers and dropouts alike may turn to.

Utilizing Jung's typology, it can be imagined that when students are more Perceiving types in a Judging environment, they tend to struggle. In the test-driven, true/false environment of public school, one who seeks to more deeply understand a subject would be less efficient, and less rewarded by grades. Studies have been conducted using the Meyers-Briggs test to study aspects of personality in education, and I am particularly interested in the experience of the INFP in what appears to be an ENTJ system. From my research, it seems that the difference between the qualities of Feeling vs. Thinking and Perceiving vs. Judging are most striking in creating learning gaps for students.

Having heard a clear message from all participants that they found teachers at the public high school to be overwhelmed by too many students, increasing workload and lack of support at school, a similar study of teachers' well-being and how they feel about the system may reveal whether the system may be oppressive at multiple levels, and not just for the students. Creating support and community *with* teachers may humanize the role of the teacher, and thereby allow for happier classrooms.

While there is increased reliability in my study due to a homogeneous population, it is by no means complete. Future studies should include participants who are of different genders and orientations, are non-white, of varied socioeconomic backgrounds, and are at different ages and levels of schooling in order to reveal a greater depth of information regarding the question of students' experience of oppression in schools. It has been shown that girls are more successful in schools than boys, at least in part because sitting still and paying attention at a young age tends to be more difficult for boys than girls. Race has clearly proven to be an issue, and there is abundant evidence that children from lower-income families are at greater risk of failing in school. Because each of these factors provide unique stressors and even trauma, they are commonly considered negative influences on students' odds for success in education. A study that excludes most of these factors yet still finds the system to be clearly oppressive is even more convincing.

Transformation is Possible

As a mother, I had the good fortune to have a second opportunity to experience my own childhood through them, and as an adult to see the world through their eyes. I witnessed their mental, physical, emotional and spiritual wholeness, and how brilliantly they learned everything they needed through love and play. I had the additional synchronicity of healing the wounds I suffered through my public school education at the same time as my son's sense of freedom, subjective wisdom, and sense of wholeness were being damaged in his public schooling. In fact, he attended one of the top public schools in California by all current measures. But we are not using the right measures to evaluate our methods. There is an invisible force that serves to repress our God-given genius, which was borne out in my research, in the voices of the young people I listened to, and through the point of view of many educators, both now and in the past.

We all know that education begins spontaneously and joyfully in children from infancy on, and continues unimpeded as long as it does not get co-opted by an adult system that doubts that we are born wired to learn. Without fully realizing it, we rely on our public school system to do a significant portion of the work of preparing our nation's children to be positive contributing members of society. But much of our public conversation about education centers on performance statistics, which misses the physical, emotional and spiritual component of learning, which are the most important features of child development. The strongest factors for success in children is to feel safe, cared about, and with a sense of belonging, to the point where, as Rebecca Goldstein said, "People want to matter, in some cases, more than they want to live." Practicing the Four C's of care, connection, community, and choice in classrooms and on campuses is a simple way to rehumanize an often institutional space, for adults and children alike.

Sadly, a large percentage of our youth will have suffered a trauma by the time they reach high school. Classrooms, especially at the lower performing level, are full of students with a wide range of issues, from intellectual impairment to emotional disorders, and we now know a high percentage of children suffer from a degree of trauma. Because of this, having a positive, loving and cooperative emotional climate at school is imperative. When kids feel that they are loved and accepted, they can relax and learn.

One of the most famous longitudinal studies ever conducted tracked a cohort of 268 Harvard graduates. These men graduated between 1941 and 1948 and had their emotional and physical health tracked for the next fifty years. The study found that love is a crucial foundation of happiness—no surprise there—and that the best predictor of a man's happiness and well-being in his seventies is the warmth of his childhood environment and the quality of his relationship with both his mother and father. George Vaillant, writing on the study, noted, "[l]ives change and things can get better...but the people who don't learn to love early pay a high price."[117]

In an ideal world, children would learn all they needed about how to love in their earliest childhood years through securely attached relationships with their parents. In the real world, the need for an extension of this attachment into school—where students spend so much of their time and forge so many important relationships—is clear. Becoming a person is a lifelong endeavor, and we continually evolve. If schools continue to teach children that knowledge is a static, concrete, and black-or-white endeavor, it limits both our progress and our possibility of becoming our highest selves in the future. Children are naturally oriented toward the future, and must be encouraged to imagine greater possibility, freely expressing their knowing with adults who care about them.

We must raise our standards of education, but not in terms of test scores or other external instruments of measurement. Our collective belief about what standards we should live up to are out of alignment with those our forefathers set for a country based on personal freedom, happiness, and love of fellow man. In his essay, "The Need to Be Maladjusted," Martin Luther King Jr. spoke of what may, in fact, need realignment:

> Modern psychology has a word that is probably used more than any other word. It is the word

---

[117] Vaillant, 2012, p. 122

"maladjusted." Now we all should seek to live a well-adjusted life in order to avoid neurotic and schizophrenic personalities. But there are some things within our social order to which I am proud to be maladjusted and to which I call upon you to be maladjusted. I never intend to adjust myself to segregation and discrimination. I never intend to adjust myself to mob rule. I never intend to adjust myself to the tragic effect of the methods of physical violence and to tragic militarism. I call upon you to be maladjusted to such things. I call upon you to be as maladjusted as Amos who in the midst of the injustices of his day cried out in words that echo across the generations. ...As maladjusted as Abraham Lincoln who had the vision to see that this nation could not exist half slave and half free. As maladjusted as Jefferson, who in the midst of an age amazingly adjusted to slavery could cry out, "All men are created equal and are endowed by their Creator with certain unalienable rights and that among these are life, liberty, and the pursuit of happiness." ...God grant that we will be so maladjusted that we will be able to go out and change our world and our civilization. And then we will be able to move from the bleak and desolate midnight of man's inhumanity to man to the bright and glittering daybreak of freedom and justice. [118]

The evidence is in: Our children are suffering, and increasingly compelled to self-destruction through drugs, alcohol, and violence. They are subject to psychological disability of all kinds, including depression, anxiety, and compulsive disorders.

---

[118] King, 1986/1992, p. 33

Happiness has become so hampered in our most academically successful students, it has become a new field of study. Stressing the importance of overcoming negative emotions and behavior, we find that positive emotions broaden the number of possibilities we process, making us more thoughtful, creative and open to new ideas. When positive emotions broaden our thoughts and behavior this way, they not only make us more creative, they help us build more intellectual, social, and physical resources we can rely upon in the future.[119]

Rather than remain within a colonized mindset, perpetuating oppression and the ensuing negative emotions and self-destructive acting out onto each new generation of young minds, we must courageously demand change toward greater humanity in schools. As adults with choice and power, we begin by recognizing the need to liberate our own thinking about self-care, and standing up for what really matters to all humans. We won't get there without bold, fearless, consistent efforts to change how we interact with each other and with our children. We have the opportunity to first listen to ourselves, take care of our needs, and then reach out to others less fortunate or empowered.

Out of all that my study's participants gleaned from their educational experiences, self-knowledge, self-acceptance, and wisdom had the most durable value to them. What allowed those factors to blossom were loving relationships. Book learning was temporary and often experienced as unpleasant and irrelevant, despite the fact that they believed these things were necessary to graduate.

---

[119] Achor, 2010, p. 44

Character can't be learned from a lecture or a book, but through relationship and overcoming challenges. When so-called academic learning can be tied to the whole self and to one's life experience, it not only deepens our connection with others and creates more lasting and enriching soul connection, but also adds to self-knowledge. It can then enhance our lives rather than oppress them. This type of education could be said to have a spiritual component, or an awareness of *anima mundi*: the soul of the world. As Ramana Maharshi said, "There will come a time when one will have to forget all that one has learned."[120] What remains after we have forgotten what we have learned is what we know of the self, and can be called wisdom.

My explorations continue down this line, with the goal of humanizing the education process for the benefit of all. A synthesis of learning about the world and learning about the self reconciles the truth of both. As I see it, an antidote for the colonized child may be found in the liberatory qualities of care, connection, community, and choice. The exercise of these qualities as a conscious stance and habitual practice opens space for learning. In shifting the weight of oppression off of our youngest citizens, we may liberate all people in the name of a more loving education process.

All this began for me with the dream of the baby girl singing, "Love, love, love." Love is where this project began, and the need for love in education is its primary finding. Our culture's uses of and attitude toward the word love have become automatic and trite, referring, most often, to

---

[120] Ramana Maharshi, 1972, p. 10

romantic love, parental love, or love between relatives or friends. This study points to a need for a bigger definition of love and a more expansive cultural conversation about love. As an expression of soul and aliveness that goes far beyond eroticism or familial ties, love is a vital cog in the machinery of learning. It is a foundational element of being human and of joining together to transform colonial mindsets and to create a strong, healthy, self-aware, liberated society.

Afterword

I FELT with profound depth Dr. Pulice's message and the impact of her words in *Listen to the Children*. Her insight and recognition of the absolute destruction of our children in an education system oblivious to the beautiful gifts of creation provided to us through our children is one that we as indigenous peoples have intimately experienced.

Our sacred children come to us with gifts and talents unique to each child, provided to fulfill a purpose in life, a life that contributes to the well-being of mankind and to the well-being of our original Mother, the Earth. Our innate "knowing" guides our path in life. It is this knowing that shapes us, guides us, protects us, and enables us to succeed in fulfilling our purpose. The systems imposed upon indigenous peoples historically and in this modern era are testament to the concerted and legalized efforts to destroy a people.

To remove us from our lands and territories to which our spirit, our minds and our physical being are innately connected, to forcibly remove our languages and culture from our children through the education systems imposed upon our people through residential schools, and to physically harm our people when we stand firm in our conviction to our responsibilities as caretakers of this Earth, this is what colonialism has done. Far from accomplishing the aim and goal of "removing the Indian from the child," the outcome has been one of destruction of lands, waters, and a lifestyle of a people decimated in the extreme.

However, the "knowing" and the Spirit within us, the flame of a powerful and proud people with a connection to this land that cannot be extinguished, was merely dampened. Today we see the resurgence of our language, our culture, our beliefs, our connection to our land, our love for each other, our love for our children. It is through this love for the gifts provided to us by our Creator that we survive and we rise. No clearer example can be provided for colonization than the attempts forced upon our peoples to forever extinguish that flame that was gifted to each of us by our Creator. No man can undo the gift of Creation.

Listen to the child, listen for his spirit, listen to his heartbeat, listen to his voice, for "out of the mouths of babes and sucklings hast thou ordained strength." The "colonized child" follows in the path imposed upon peoples of our land, a system designed to fulfill a singular purpose, that of industrialization for the benefit of those who rise to the top. Listen to the child, the child will guide what is meant to be, that was intended to be, and what will be. Within each child is the history of his family from time immemorial; teachings, songs, ceremony, experience, all of which was provided for the benefit of the generations yet to come. All that is needed for learning is to listen to our "knowing," listen to our heart, and trust in our Spirit.

Wopida, Mitakuye Owasin.

—Katherine Whitecloud, Knowledge Keeper, elder, community leader, Wipazoka Wakpa Dakota Nation

References

Achor, S. (2010). *The happiness advantage.* New York, NY, Crown.

Arendt, H. (1968). *Totalitarianism.* New York, NY: Harcourt Brace Jovanovich.

Barry, K. (2010). *Developing a critical consciousness of authority while following the call of vocation: A study of lessons learned from women of the immaculate heart community* (Doctoral dissertation). Retrieved from UMI (3447656)

Beesdo, K., Knappe, S., & Pine, D. S. (2009). Anxiety and anxiety disorders in children and adolescents: developmental issues and implications for DSM-V. *Psychiatric Clinics,* 32(3), 483-524.

Bentz, V. M., & Shapiro, J. (1998). *Mindful inquiry in social research.* Thousand Oaks, CA: Sage.

Bloomberg, L., & Volpe, M. (2008). *Completing your qualitative dissertation: A roadmap from beginning to end.* Los Angeles, CA: Sage.

Boal, A. (1979). *Theater of the oppressed.* New York, NY: Theater Communications Group.

Bowles, S., & Gintis, H. (1977). *Schooling in capitalist America: Educational reform and the contradictions of economic life.* New York, NY: Basic Books.

Brown, G. I. (1977). *Human teaching for human learning: An introduction to confluent education.* Dallas, PA: Offset Paperback. (Original work published 1971)

Cannella, G., & Kincheloe, J. (2002). *Kidsworld: Childhood studies, global perspective, and education.* New York, NY: Peter Lang.

Centers for Disease Control and Prevention (2016). Understanding school violence. Retrieved from https://www.cdc.gov/violenceprevention/pdf/ School_Violence_Fact_Sheet-a.pdf

Cobb, E. (1977). *The ecology of imagination in childhood.* Dallas, TX: Spring.

Coppin, J., & Nelson, E. (2005). *The art of inquiry: A depth psychological perspective* (2nd ed.). New York, NY: Spring.

Creswell, J. (2014). *Research design: Qualitative, quantitative, and mixed method approaches* (4th ed.). Los Angeles, CA: Sage.

Douglass, B., & Moustakas, C. (1985). Heuristic inquiry: The internal search to know. *Journal of Humanistic Psychology, 25*(3), 39-55.

Eaton, D. K., Kann, L., Kinchen, S., Shanklin, S., Ross, J., Hawkins, J., & Wechsler, H. (2008). Youth risk behavior surveillance—United States, 2007. *MMWR Surveillance Summaries, 57*(SS04), 1-131. Retrieved from http://www.cdc.gov/MMWR/preview/mmwrhtml/ss5704a1.htm

Finkelhor, D., Turner, H. A., Shattuck, A., & Hamby, S. L. (2015). Prevalence of childhood exposure to violence, crime, and abuse: Results from the national survey of children's exposure to violence. JAMA pediatrics, 169(8), 746-754

Freire, P. (2005). *Pedagogy of the oppressed* (W. B. Ramos, Trans.). New York, NY: Continuum. (Original work published 1970)

Fromm, E. (2006). *The art of loving.* New York, NY: Harper Perennial Modern Classics. (Original work published 1956)

Gatto, T. (2005). *Dumbing us down.* Gabriola Island, BC, CAN: New Society.

Ginsburg, K., & Jablow, M. (2011). *Building resilience in children and teens* (2nd ed.). Elk Grove Village, IL: American Academy of Pediatrics.

Harvard University (n.d.). Center on the developing child. *Toxic Stress*. Retrieved from https://developingchild.harvard.edu/science/key-concepts/toxic-stress

Hawe, P., & Shiell, A. (2000). Social capital and health promotion: A review. *Social Science & Medicine, 51*(6), 871-885.

Hillman, J. (1992). *Re-visioning psychology*. New York, NY: Harper Perennial. (Original work published 1975)

Holt, J. (1967). *How children fail*. New York, NY: New American Library.

hooks, b. (1994). *Teaching to transgress: Education as the practice of freedom*. New York, NY: Routledge.

hooks, b. (2001). *All about love: New visions*. New York, NY: Perennial.

Horosko, M. (2002). *Martha Graham: The evolution of her dance theory and training*. Gainesville, FL: University Press of Florida.

Iacoboni, M. (2009). Imitation, empathy, and mirror neurons. *Annual Review of Psychology, 60*, 653-670.

Jung, C. G. (1954). The gifted child. In R. F. C. Hull (Trans.), *The collected works of C. G. Jung* (CW 17, pp. 135-145). Princeton, NJ: Princeton University Press. (Original work published 1946)

Kabat-Zinn, J. (2005). *Coming to our senses: Healing ourselves and the world through mindfulness*. New York, NY: Hyperion Books.

Kesner, J. (2005, May). *Gifted children's relationships with teachers*. Retrieved from https://www.researchgate.net/profile/John_Kesner/publications

Kessler, R. (2000). *The soul of education: Helping students find connection, compassion, and character at school*. Alexandria, VA: Association for Supervision and Curriculum Development.

Kincheloe, J., & McLaren, P. (2003). Rethinking critical theory and qualitative research. In N. K. Denzin & Y. S. Lincoln (Eds.), *The landscape of qualitative research: Theories and issues* (pp. 433-488). Thousand Oaks, CA: Sage.

King, M. L., Jr. (1986). *I have a dream: Writings and speeches that changed the world*. San Francisco, CA: Harper Collins.

Kohn, Alfie. (2000). *The case against standardized testing*. Portsmouth, NH: Heinemann.

Levine, M. (2012). *Teach your children well: Parenting for authentic success.* New York, NY: HarperCollins.

Lewis, P. (1968, June 6). London, UK, BBC interview with John Lennon and Victor Spinetti [interview]. Retrieved from http://www.beatlesbible. com/1968/06/06/bbc-interview-with-john-lennon-and-victor-spinetti/

Liedloff, J. (1977). *The continuum concept: In search of happiness lost (Classics in human development).* Cambridge, MA: Perseus Books. (Original work published 1975)

Maharshi, R. (1972). *The spiritual teaching of Ramana Maharshi.* Boston, MA: Shambhala.

Montessori, M. (1949). *The absorbent mind* (Vol. 1). Lulu. com.

Mayes, C. (2007). *Inside education: Depth psychology in teaching and learning.* Madison, WI: Atwood.

Miller, J. (1974). Rediscovering the rhetoric of imagination. *College Composition and Communication, 25,* 5, 360-367. Retrieved from https://eric. ed.gov/?id=EJ110784

Miller, A. (1981). *Drama of the gifted child: The search for the true self* (R. Ward, Trans.). New York, NY: Basic Books. (Original work published 1979)

Mintz, S. (2004). *Huck's raft: A history of American childhood.* Cambridge, MA: Belknap Press.

Musselman, F. (1914). Play as fundamental in education. *Francis W. Parker School Year Book, 3,* 25-36.

National Institute of Mental Health (2017). Statistics on major depression. Retrieved from https://www.nimh.nih.gov/health/statistics/major-depression.shtml

National Institute of Mental Health (2017). Statistics on suicide. Retrieved from www.nimh.nih.gov/health/statistics/suicide.shtml

National Resource Center on ADHD (n.d.). Data and statistics. *General Prevalence.* Retrieved from www.chadd.org/understanding-adhd/about-adhd/data-and-statistics/general-prevalence.aspx

Palmer, P. J. (1998). *The courage to teach.* San Francisco, CA: Jossey-Bass.

Papadopoulos, R. (2002). The other other: When the exotic other subjugates the familiar other. *Journal of Analytical Psychology, 47,* 163-188.

Parker J. D. A., Creque, R. E., Barnhart, D. L., Irons, J., Majeski, S. A., Wood, L. M., … Hogan, M. J. (2004). Academic achievement in high school: Does emotional intelligence matter? *Personality and Individual Differences, 37,* 1321-1330.

Pastor, P. N., Reuben, C. A., Duran, C. R., & Hawkins, L. D. (2015). Association between Diagnosed ADHD and Selected Characteristics among Children Aged 4-17 Years: United States, 2011-2013. NCHS Data Brief. Number 201. *Centers for Disease Control and Prevention.*

Pearce, J. C. (1977). *The magical child.* New York, NY: Plume Books.

Prout, A., & James, A. (1997*). Constructing and reconstructing childhood: Contemporary issues in the sociological study of childhood* (2nd ed.). Bristol, PA: Falmer Press.

Pulice, S. (2009). *The experience of mutuality and hierarchy in learning for children.* Unpublished manuscript. Pacifica Graduate Institute, Carpinteria, CA.

Pulice, S. (2010). *Re-membering the natural child.* Unpublished manuscript. Pacifica Graduate Institute, Carpinteria, CA.

Putnam, R. D. (2010). *Bowling alone: The collapse and revival of American community.* New York, NY: Simon & Schuster.

Ravitch, D. (2011). *Death and life of the great American school system: How testing and choice are undermining education.* New York, NY: Basic Books.

Riley, P. (2011). *Attachment theory and teacher-student relationship: A practical guide for teachers, teacher*

educators and school leaders. New York, NY:
Routledge.

Sacks, V., Murphey, D., & Moore, K. (2014) Child
trends. *Adverse Childhood Experiences: National and
State Level Prevalence.* Retrieved from https://www.
childtrends.org/wp-content/uploads/2014/07/
Brief-adverse-childhood-experiences_FINAL.pdf

Santa Barbara Middle School. Mission Statement. (n.d.).
Retrieved from http://www.sbms.org/03about/
mission.html

Sardello, R. (1996). *Love and the soul: Creating a future for
earth.* San Francisco, CA: Harper Perennial.

Schulman-Lorenz, H., & Watkins, M. (2003). Depth
psychology and colonialism: Individuation, seeing
through, and liberation. *Quadrant, 33*(1), 11-32.

Selig, J. (2007). *Phenomenology of depth psychological cultural
work, DP 880.* Lecture conducted from Pacifica
Graduate Institute, Carpinteria, CA.

Shepherd, P. (2010). *New self, new world: Recovering our senses
in the twenty-first century.* Berkeley, CA: North
Atlantic Books.

Smith, H. G. (2003). *Indigenous struggle for the transformation
of education and schooling.* Retrieved from
_____ www.ankn.uaf.edu

Substance Abuse and Mental Health Services
Administration. (n.d). *Trauma-informed approach and
trauma-specific interventions.* Retrieved from https://
www.samhsa.gov/nctic/trauma-interventions

Spurr, D. (1993). *The rhetoric of empire: Colonial discourse in
journalism, travel writing, and imperial administration.*
Durham, NC: Duke University Press.

Taylor, C., Appiah, K. A., Haberman, J., Rockefeller, S.
C., Walzer, M., & Wolf, S. (1994). In A. Gutman
(Ed.), *Multiculturalism: Examining the politics of
recognition.* Princeton, NJ: Princeton University
Press.

The National Child Traumatic Stress Network. (n.d.)
Retrieved from http://www.nctsn.org/

Tough, P. (2012). *How children succeed.* New York, NY:
Houghton Mifflin.

US Department of Education. (n.d,). The department's
FY 2012-2013 priority performance goals.
Retrieved from http://www2.ed.gov/about/
overview/focus/goals.html

Vaillant, G. (2012). *Triumphs and experience: The men of the
Harvard Grant study.* Cambridge, MA: Belknap
Press of Harvard University Press.

Visser, S. N., Lesesne, C. A., & Perou, R. (2007) National
estimates and factors associated with medication

treatment for childhood attention deficit/ hyperactivity disorder. *Pediatrics: Official Journal of the American Academy of Pediatrics.119*, S99-S106.

Voight, A., Austin, G., & Hanson, T. (2013). *A climate for academic success: How school climate distinguishes schools that are beating the achievement odds* (Report summary). San Francisco, CA: WestEd.

Waldorf Education. (n.d.). Retrieved from https:// waldorfeducation.org/waldorf_education

Wallin, D. (2007). *Attachment in psychotherapy.* New York, NY: Guilford Press.

Ward, T. (2003). *Reawakening indigenous sensibilities in the western psyche* (Doctoral dissertation). Retrieved from Proquest. (UMI No. 3144564)

Wickelgren, I. (2012, November 27). *How social emotional learning could harm our kids* (Web log comment). Retrieved from http://blogs.scientificamerican. com/streamsof-consciousness

Wilkinson, M. (2006). *Coming into mind: The mind-brain relationship: A Jungian clinical perspective.* New York, NY: Routledge.

Woolfolk, R. L., Sass, L. A., & Messer, S. B. (1988). Introduction to hermeneutics. In S. B. Messer, L. A. Sass, & R. L. Woolfolk (Eds.), *Hermeneutics and psychological theory: Interpretive perspectives on personality, psychotherapy, and psychopathology* (pp. 2-26). New Brunswick, NJ: Rutgers University Press.

Zinns, J., Bloodworth, M., Weissberg, R., & Walberg, H. (2007). The scientific base linking social and emotional learning to school success. *Journal of Educational Psychological Consultation, 17*(2-3), 191-210.

ABOUT THE AUTHOR

Stacy Pulice, Ph.D., is the founder of The Art of Rehumanizing, sharing the perspective that kindness and human connection brings out the best in people. A mother of three, her current research centers around love, healing and emotional safety in schools. Stacy has an unquenchable thirst to integrate the many facets of human existence—from authoring think pieces on increasing community to launching a public school teaching garden fostering connection to the soil for teens. She has a deep belief in the power of self-care as an act of resistance to oppression, and seeks to expand simple practices in all aspects of life to improve our human experience. For more than twenty years, Stacy has served on numerous boards committed to fostering emotional intelligence in education.

Visit her websites:

www.listentothechildrenbook.com

www.theartofrehumanizing.com

CPSIA information can be obtained
at www.ICGtesting.com
Printed in the USA
FSHW04n0938060418
46415FS